SPOOKED IN
SEATTLE

AMERICA'S
HAUNTED ROAD TRIP

Spooked in Seattle: A Haunted Handbook

For further information, contact the publisher at:
Clerisy Press
An imprint of AdventureKEEN
306 Greenup Street
Covington, KY 41011
www.clerisypress.com

Library of Congress Cataloging-in-Publication Data
  Allison, Ross.
    Spooked in Seattle : a haunted handbook / Ross Allison. — 1st ed.
      p. cm.
    ISBN-13: 978-1-57860-501-9 (pbk.); ISBN 978-1-57860-502-6 (ebook)
    ISBN-10: 1-57860-501-6 (pbk.); ISBN 978-1-57860-624-5 (hardcover)
    1. Ghosts—Washington—Seattle. 2. Haunted places—Washington—Seattle. I. Title.

    BF1472.U6A445 2011
    133.109797'772--dc23
                                    2011027311

Distributed by Publishers Group West
Printed in the United States of America
First edition, first printing

Editor: Donna Poehner
Cover design: Scott McGrew
Text design: Annie Long
Cover and interior photos provided by the author

SPOOKED IN SEATTLE

A HAUNTED HANDBOOK

ROSS ALLISON

clerisy press

Ghost (gōst) *noun.* The soul of a dead person, a disembodied spirit imagined, usually as a vague, shadowy, or evanescent form, as wandering among or haunting living persons.

Synonyms: Apparition, phantom, phantasm, wraith, revenant; shade, spook. Ghost, specter, spirit all refer to the disembodied soul of a person. A ghost is the soul or spirit of a deceased person, which appears or otherwise makes its presence known to the living: the ghost of a drowned child. A specter is a ghost or apparition of more or less weird, unearthly, or terrifying aspect: a frightening specter. Spirit is often interchangeable with ghost but may mean a supernatural being, usually with an indication of good or malign intent toward human beings: the spirit of a friend; an evil spirit.

Source: **Dictionary.com**

THIS BOOK IS DEAD-ICATED TO

JAM,
Without you, this project would not have been completed,
just as I would not have been completed without you.
110709

My Dear Great Grandmother,
Thank you for the unconditional love and support.
I love you.

Mother,
Thanks for opening my eyes at a young age to
a world stranger than the one in my head.
I love you.

Mark,
You've supported me for many years as
I followed my dreams.
Thank you.
I hope your dreams come true as much as mine did.

AGHOST
Without all of you members past and present,
this book would have never been made.
Thank you for all of your support.

To all the ghost hunters out there—
be safe and be honest.
The truth will be found.

TABLE OF CONTENTS

ABOUT THIS BOOK

This guide presents many locations throughout Seattle that are believed to be haunted, claim to have ghosts, or have undergone investigation. We cannot say for certain if these claims are 100 percent true—that's for you to decide if you dare to venture to them in search of the dead. Just remember that not all these sites will support your personal investigation into the unknown. If you do plan to investigate, please be respectful of the property and the dead.

This book is broken down into sections based on Seattle's neighborhoods with corresponding addresses to make finding them easier. Whether you use your GPS or Mapquest.com, or some other means of finding them, we hope you enjoy your adventure into the unknown.

The neighborhood maps in this book provide number markers. Those numbers coincide with the location and story in that chapter. Pretty easy, huh?

Happy Hunting!

 An AGHOST investigation was done at this site

GHOSTS TODAY

Whether you believe in the world of the spirits or not, the belief in ghosts has jumped quite a bit since 2005. Today, with so many TV shows and movies featuring true belief in ghosts, many skeptics have become believers or at least are more open to the idea that something may very well be out there.

When Spiritualism was big in the 1800s, it was focused on mediums, psychic impressions, and entertainment. Not a lot of science was involved. But there were groups researching the paranormal phenomena, including Harry Price, Thomas Edison, or even London's Ghost Club, which was founded in 1862 along with Society for Psychical Research (SPR).

Now we tend to find the complete opposite, where most people want to find a scientific answer to what seems to be occurring at haunted sites. Every day new tools are developed in hopes of offering a new view into some of the strange happenings. With EMF detectors, recorders, and cameras in hand, the ghost hunter treks to hundreds of haunted sites in search for the unknown. Will their hard work and efforts pay off?

The truth will be found.

TOP 10 QUESTIONS ABOUT G H O S T S

1. *Are ghosts and hauntings real?*

The belief in ghosts continues to grow. Many believe in the possibility of ghosts and in what people claim to be hauntings or ghosts. But don't take my word for it. The best way to find truth in anything is to make the discovery for yourself. This book might help you find that unique encounter with the unknown and help you decide if are ghosts real.

2. *What is a Ghost?*

There are many different beliefs regarding what a ghost is, but the most common is that the soul of a dead person still lingers among the living. In some cases the soul or energy can interact with the living or just play out a certain event over and over again without any interaction.

3. *How do you know if you have a ghost in your home?*

There are many different types of phenomena labeled as a ghost haunting. Here are a few to guide you: strange noises that cannot be explained; cold spots; objects that disappear never to be found or that move to different locations without explanation; doors and windows open or close on their own; electrical problems, or lights and appliances that turn on and off on their own. You may also see shadows, strange lights, or even transparent figures moving around the property.

4. *Can a building be haunted?*

The common belief is that ghosts can attach themselves to a person, place, or object. This can include a home, business, or land. Some also believe that a location may have the ability to record past events, and these events can be played out for unsuspecting guests.

5. *Why does a ghost haunt?*

There are many reasons a ghost may choose to haunt a location. This may be a place where the ghost lived or where a tragic event happened to her. Somebody the ghost loves or knows might be on the property. The ghost has a message to pass on, unfinished business, or he might not even know he has passed on and so still goes about his everyday life.

6. *Can animals be ghosts?*

There have been many reports of animals seen as ghosts, especially pets. Some people claim to hear growling or barking from a dog, or hissing or meowing from a cat. Some people can feel animals crawling into bed with them, and, of course, there are claims of seeing a deceased pet or animal on the property.

7. *What is a poltergeist?*

There are many misunderstandings about the differences between a ghost and a poltergeist. The common mistake people make is that they think if there is any type of physical activity, such as moving objects or physical harm to a person, it must be a poltergeist. This is not true. A true poltergeist case is focused on what we call an agent, which is someone who emits unknown PK (psychokinesis) ability—the ability to move things with the mind. In a poltergeist case, the agent tends to be a child going through puberty or stressful conditions, or a woman going through menopause, who will unknowingly cause physical disturbance in their environment.

8. *What is a residual haunting?*

It is reported that 80 percent of hauntings are residual energy, where energy will repeat itself over and over like a trapped memory or a repeating movie sequence. This "energy" is not intelligent, so it will not react to the living or their environment. In cases where people see apparitions walk through walls, we often find after research there was formerly a door in that location. In some cases, even the living can leave residual energy behind.

9. *Can you get rid of ghosts?*

Yes and no. In most cases dealing with residual activity, the answer is no unless you can find the source that feeds the energy and remove it. Otherwise, these energies will continue to play themselves out. When it comes to an intelligent haunting, it may be possible to get rid of the ghost. The best way to banish an unwanted spirit is to make contact. If contact is made, then you might be able to convince the ghost to move on. But remember, you are dealing with something that has free will, and if it chooses to stay, you may have a bigger challenge ahead of you.

10. *Who ya gonna call?*

At a time when ghost hunting is becoming more popular, you may find many ghost hunting groups in your area willing to assist. You tend to find different types of groups and people involved. There are the thrill seekers, those who want to experience what they see on popular ghost hunting shows and don't really follow through with the re-search needed. Then you have the groups that are really not educated in the field; their intent is true, but they may not be able to offer you the service you seek.

When choosing a group to help identify your encounters, first research the groups you have to choose from, asking: How long have they been in service? Is there training involved? Do they charge a fee? What services do they provide? How much experience do they have? You can always ask for references as well. It is always good to get a second opinion.

SEATTLE'S TOP 10 MOST HAUNTED

This list is based on research and personal encounters and consists of what could very well be Seattle's most haunted hot spots. When it comes to ghosts and ghost hunting, you'll find it really is all about being at the right place at the right time. So there is no guarantee that you will encounter a ghost or any paranormal activity. When people report their encounters, they tend to be on the location at least eight hours a day. So their chances of running into a ghost are much higher. This also applies to ghost hunting. Ghost hunters find that only one out of ten cases provides evidence of a possible haunting. So keep this in mind as you visit the locations in this book.

1. The Seattle Underground (p. 15)
2. Butterworth's (p. 82)
3. Harvard Exit Theatre (p. 124)
4. The Arctic Club (p. 19)
5. Amazon.com Building (p. 98)
6. The Moore Theater (p. 104)
7. Georgetown Castle (p. 165)
8. Frye's Hotel (p. 36)
9. University Heights (p. 160)
10. Comet Lodge Cemetery (p. 168)

SPOOKED IN
SEATTLE

1. Seattle History

It seems all major cities have their share of death, murder, and mayhem. And with these events slowly unfold the stories of the strange, the bizarre, and—my personal favorite—the haunting tales of ghosts that roam within the city's gates. So it doesn't surprise me that Seattle, the Emerald City, has its fair share of ghosts, just like any other city in the United States.

Okay, so Seattle isn't riddled with tons of history, due to its late birth in 1851, when the first white party took settlement in what we call Alki Point (or better known as West Seattle) across the Elliot Bay. This was to be called "New York, Alki," but this land was too exposed to the elements, and so after the first winter, the settlers packed up and tried their luck across the bay at what is now known as Seattle. But its first name was Duwamps, meaning "tide flats" among the natives. Since Seattle got such a late start, there wasn't much opportunity for too many tragic events to occur as in older cities across the country. However, Seattle was inhabited by others before the white people took over the land. For 10,000 years, the Suquamish and Duwamish tribes walked these lands, fished the waters, and hunted the woods. There were wars among tribes, destructive fires, and death among their people. So it's clearly their history that haunts Seattle's past. The Native Americans strongly believed in the Great Spirit. In fact, it was their belief in all spirits that guided them to a better life and understanding of all things around them, leaving us with a history we still need to learn from.

FIRST SETTLEMENT OF SEATTLE

BATTLE OF SEATTLE

The morning of January 26, 1856, Seattle was attacked by the Native Americans. At the time, Seattle was a settlement in the Washington Territory that had recently named itself after Chief Seattle. The *Decatur*, a U.S. Navy ship, was docked in Elliot Bay in anticipation of trouble with local Indians, but also as a deterrent against Native Americans from Vancouver Island who regularly raided both Native American and white settlements. In addition, warnings and inside information from Chief Seattle; his daughter, Princess Angeline; and Curly Jim, another local Native American, allowed Seattle's fifty or so white residents to prepare for the attack. When the battle broke out it only lasted a single day and was reported to have only two causalities among the settlers. One was a man remembered only by the name of Wilson, who was watching the battle from the Felker Hotel's verandah long enough to be hit and killed by a bullet fired from the forest. The other was an imprudent spectator who looked out from the temporarily opened door of one of the blockhouses. This is a pretty amazing count when it was reported that 160 men were dodging bullets for over ten hours that day. Plus the range of the *Decatur's* guns kept the Native Americans at a distance. However the loss for the Native Americans was estimated at twenty-eight dead and eighty wounded among the one thousand fighting. At first the loss to the Native American's side wasn't known, due to the belief that the Native women were in charge of collecting the dead and wounded so none would be found. Afterwards, Snoqualmie Chief Pat Kanim offered a bounty for the heads of those who attacked Seattle ($80 for a chief and $20 for a warrior), and historian Clarence Bagley states, "During the month of February 1856, several invoices of these ghastly trophies were received and

BATTLE OF SEATTLE

sent to Olympia." The cause of the battle was land. As more and more settlers came to Seattle, more Native Americans were made to move to other ground, taking them away from their waters and hunting grounds.

See also: Mother Damnable in this section

CHIEF SEATTLE

Chief Noah Sealth (See-atch) was a leader of the Suquamish and Duwamish Native American tribes. Born around 1786, he died June 7, 1866, on the Suquamish reservation at Port Madison, Washington.

Like his father before him, Sealth was chief of the Suquamish tribe that settled on Bainbridge Island, and his mother was the daughter of a Duwamish chief. The Duwamish tribe settled on a small river in southwest Seattle across from the Puget Sound area.

History states that Chief Seattle was known to be a brave warrior—courageous, daring, and a great leader in his battles. He gained control over six tribes and pursued a working friendship with the Europeans like his father had done.

Chief Seattle was befriended by Seattle pioneer David Swinson Maynard, also known as "Doc." Their friendship built the alliance between the Native Americans, and it also led to the naming of the city of Seattle. At the time the city was called Duwamps, named after the local Duwamish tribe. When Doc mentioned his interest in naming the city after Sealth in honor of the chief and his people, the chief was outraged due to the belief that if you speak the name of a deceased ancestor, it will disturb their spiritual rest. They worked out the problem, however, because the white

CHIEF SEATTLE

settlers couldn't pronounce his name correctly, which is why we say Seattle and not Sealth. Also, Doc didn't think the chief would live too much longer and sweetened the deal with offering him a sum of fifty dollars for every year he lived. Surprisingly, the chief lived another thirty years, making it a sweeter deal for himself.

Besides the many other great things Chief Seattle has done, he was known for his poetic way with words. In one famous speech in December of 1854, Sealth addressed an outdoor gathering of Seattle locals on developing relations with the local Native Americans. Chief Seattle says in his native Lushootseed Language:

> *To us the ashes of our ancestors are sacred and their resting place is hallowed ground. You wander far from the graves of your ancestors and seemingly without regret. Your religion was written upon tablets of stone by the iron finger of your God so that you could not forget. The Red Man could never comprehend or remember it. Our religion is the traditions of our ancestors—the dreams of our old men, given them in solemn hours of the night by the Great Spirit; and the visions of our sachems, and is written in the hearts of our people.*

> *Your dead cease to love you and the land of their nativity as soon as they pass the portals of the tomb and wander away beyond the stars. They are soon forgotten and never return. Our dead never forget this beautiful world that gave them being. They still love its verdant valleys, its murmuring rivers, its magnificent mountains, sequestered vales and verdant-lined lakes and bays, and ever yearn in tender fond affection over the lonely-hearted living, and often return from the happy hunting ground to visit, guide, console, and comfort them.*

> *A few more moons, a few more winters, and not one of the descendants of the mighty hosts that once moved over this broad land or lived in happy homes, protected by the Great Spirit, will remain to mourn over the graves of a people once more powerful and hopeful than yours. But why should I mourn at the untimely fate of my people? Tribe follows tribe, and nation follows nation, like the waves of the sea. It is the order of nature, and regret is useless. Your time of decay may be distant, but it will surely come, for even the White Man whose God walked and talked with him as friend to friend, cannot be exempt from the common destiny. We may be brothers after all. We will see.*

We will ponder your proposition, and when we decide we will let you know. But should we accept it, I here and now make this condition that we will not be denied the privilege without molestation of visiting at any time the tombs of our ancestors, friends, and children. Every part of this soil is sacred in the estimation of my people. Every hillside, every valley, every plain and grove, has been hallowed by some sad or happy event in days long vanished. Even the rocks, which seem to be dumb and dead as they swelter in the sun along the silent shore, thrill with memories of stirring events connected with the lives of my people, and the very dust upon which you now stand responds more lovingly to their footsteps than yours, because it is rich with the blood of our ancestors, and our bare feet are conscious of the sympathetic touch. Our departed braves, fond mothers, glad, happy-hearted maidens, and even the little children who lived here and rejoiced here for a brief season, will love these somber solitudes and at eventide they greet shadowy returning spirits. And when the last Red Man shall have perished, and the memory of my tribe shall have become a myth among the White Men, these shores will swarm with the invisible dead of my tribe, and when your children's children think themselves alone in the field, the store, the shop, upon the highway, or in the silence of the pathless woods, they will not be alone. In all the earth there is no place dedicated to solitude. At night when the streets of your cities and villages are silent and you think them deserted, they will throng with the returning hosts that once filled them and still love this beautiful land. The White Man will never be alone. Let him be just and deal kindly with my people, for the dead are not altogether powerless."

These are truly powerful words of a poet and a very wise man. This was only a portion of his moving speech that was to open the minds of the white man. But, unfortunately, most white people didn't speak his language, and it wasn't until some years later that Dr. Henry A. Smith translated it into an English version.

Clarence B. Bagley reprinted a slightly altered version in his 1929 *History of King County Washington*. Bagley appended a new close without explanation or attribution:

"Dead—I say? There is no death. Only a change of worlds."

Whether or not Chief Seattle would have said this, they are words truly inspired by a great man, whose spirit will live forever in the heart of Seattle.

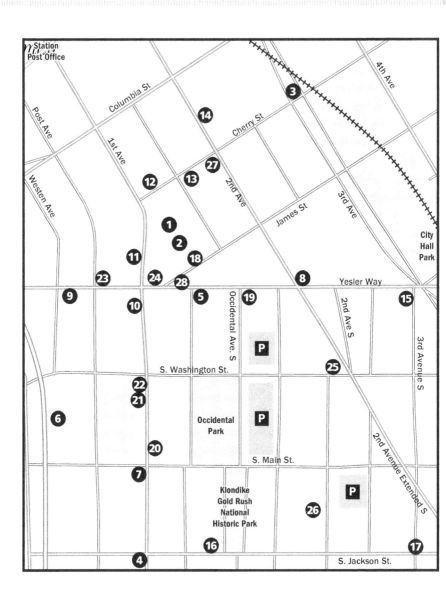

2. PIONEER SQUARE

Pioneer Square is the birthplace of Seattle and may be thought of as the city's first neighborhood. With its tumultuous history, this area may also be one of Seattle's most haunted. Conflict between Native Americans and the pioneer settlers, the Great Seattle Fire, and even more recent tragedies have left their mark on this neighborhood. From untimely deaths to brutal murders and hangings of innocent people, Pioneer Square has its share of pain.

Along with the neighborhood's rich history, this area holds a number of attractions. As the home of Seattle's nightlife, Pioneer Square has a vast collection of art galleries, shops, bars, and restaurants. It is also one of the most architecturally diverse neighborhoods in the United States. Some of the must-sees of the area include the Pioneer Square Totem Pole, the "Sinking Ship" parking garage, and the statue of Chief Seattle.

MAP MARKERS

1. Doc Maynard's Public House
2. The Underground Tour
3. Arctic Club
4. Mother Damnable
5. Merchants Café
6. OK Hotel
7. Star Bar
8. The Smith Tower
9. Pioneer Square Hotel
10. Chocolate Factory
11. Mutual Life Building
12. DeNunzio's Restaurant
13. Mystery Book Shop
14. United Way Building
15. Frye's Hotel
16. Temple Billiards
17. Joseph and the Chuckhole
18. Pioneer Building
19. Interurban Building
20. Megan Mary Olander Florists
21. The Central
22. J&M Café
23. Marcus' Martini Heaven
24. Dutch Ned
25. The Double Header
26. 88 Keys
27. Broderick Building
28. The Seattle Hotel

GREAT SEATTLE FIRE

On June 6, 1889, John E. Back, a worker in Victor Clairmont's cabinetmaking shop near the old Front Street and Madison Avenue, was making glue in a hot glue pot. The glue boiled over starting a fire on the shop's wooden floor. The fire soon spread to the wood chips and turpentine covering the floor. But, the small shop fire combined with many other elements to create the tragedy of the Great Seattle Fire.

The tragedy of the great fire might not have happened if . . .

If the neighboring building wasn't a supply shop storing ammo, gun powder, and dynamite.

If the fire hadn't spread to a warehouse that had received fifty barrels of whiskey just an hour earlier.

If the fire chief had not been out of town at a firefighters' convention in San Francisco.

If the fire trucks had not gotten stuck in the mud flats.

If a poor water-pump system hadn't failed to maintain water pressure for the firefighters' hoses.

GREAT SEATTLE FIRE

If (unbelievably true) the city officials hadn't asked young men to use dynamite to blow up the buildings surrounding the fire. Granted, they hoped to contain the fire by removing some of these structures, but these young men were blowing up buildings already on fire, spreading burning rubble.

All of these possibilities contributed to the city's destruction as Seattle burned to the ground in just twelve hours! John Back snuck out of Seattle the next day unaware the hero he had become. This was a chance for the pioneers to fix all their city problems. So the citizens were back at work rebuilding their city the very next day. The fire leveled the city, giving the settlers a chance to rebuild and correct many of the mistakes they had made when building the first city. They could raise the city above sea level, correcting the drainage problems they had been living with for too long.

But starting over doesn't mean people will do things correctly the second time around. With the conflict of how to rebuild, business owners and city officials could not agree on the new outline or direction for the city. So, Seattle's complicated redesign was the consequence of two separate groups building the city at the same time, which resulted in raised streets and steep sidewalks.

DEATH AND HANGINGS

In a town where law and order had little control of troubled townsfolk, many unfortunate things occurred. Here are a few stories that show how mass hysteria and corruption contributed to the tales of death and murder. A few of these events very well may have left spirits behind to haunt our city streets.

April 1854—The body of a tradesman from Pennsylvania was found in a shallow grave on the beach of Lake Union. Three Native Americans were accused of the crime. Later that day, angry townspeople were able to retrieve two of the natives and proceeded to drag them to the corner of First and Main where a group of men quickly tried them and found them guilty. Then the mob hung the two from the tree nearby. Later a third Native American was able to have a fair trial, and it was discovered that he was an innocent man. So it was believed the other two men were most likely innocent as well.

October 1881—Seattle police officer David Sires was having a beer at James Smith Saloon, on Second and Washington when a gun went off. Even though he wasn't in uniform, he investigated. When he exited the saloon, many witness pointed to a man who was running away. Office Sires pursued on foot and was able catch up to the gunman at the corner of Third and Yesler. At this time the running man warned Sires to stay back, but Sires continued pursuing him without identifying himself. The man shot Sires in the throat. At this moment a woman stepped out to see what the commotion was and found the officer lying on the ground and the gunman running away. Officer Sires died a few days later, but only after he admitted he had failed to announce himself as he gave chase. He became Seattle's first police officer killed in the line of duty. The gunman was later identified as Ben Payne and was arrested after claiming the shooting was an accident. He had thought that Officer Sires was a robber. Payne was placed in jail until a trial could be set. Payne remained in custody until January 1882.

January 1882—George Reynolds, while strolling at Third and Marion, was robbed by two men at gunpoint. Refusing to hand over his belongings, he proceeded to go for his revolver only moments too late as the two gunmen both opened fire on him. George died from gunshot wounds to the chest, and the robbers hid as the citizens of Seattle began a citywide search for them. Four hours later both men were caught, but the locals wanted to take matters into their own hands. They took the two gunmen from the officers and dragged them to the site on James Street between First and Second, which is now Pioneer Square Park. There they hung the two men from the trees. It was then that a member of the mob shouted out for the hanging of Ben Payne. The crowd, still hungry for blood, stormed the jail and proceeded to fight off Sheriff Wyckoff and pull Payne from his cell. They then dragged him to the hanging trees where the two gunmen still swung. Payne cried out his innocence and stated to the mob, "You hang me, and you will hang an innocent man." They hung him. It was said that the mob kept a reminder of the hangings to warn future criminals of what could happen.

June 1901—G.O. Guy drugstore at Second and Yesler was the site of an infamous shootout between former Police Chief William L. Meredith and John Considine, owner of the People's Theater, a "box house," which provided small acts, like magic shows, dancing, and occasionally sexual favors in the back rooms.

Feuding began between the two after charges were brought against Meredith for corruption, only after Considine would not give in to payoffs. Meredith then had to resign under the pressure of the investigation. Meredith proceeded to accuse Considine for impregnating a seventeen-year-old performer who worked in Considine's box house.

G.O. GUY DRUGSTORE

The morning of the shootout, Considine, furious over the allegations, went to Meredith's lawyer to inform him that if Meredith would not retract the claim, he was ready to sue for libel. Considine was told that the town was not big enough for both him and Meredith. Hearing that, Considine called his brother and then armed himself.

It was apparent that Meredith was waiting for Considine. Fully armed, he watched Considine and his brother approach the drugstore. He soon followed with a sawed-off shotgun in hand. Outside the store, Meredith shot John Considine in the arm. Considine stumbled into the store with Meredith following after him. The next shot grazed Considine in the back of the neck, striking the arm of a messenger boy at the soda fountain. Meredith then dropped the shotgun and went for his revolver. Considine jumped Meredith, wrestled him toward the entrance while calling out for help from his brother. Tom Considine grabbed Meredith's shotgun and struck Meredith in the head, fracturing his skull. At this time police arrived, including Sheriff Cudihee. Tom then grabbed one of their guns and aimed at them, yelling, "Stand back, you sons of bitches!"

Meanwhile, John Considine drew his gun on the wounded Meredith while he possibly was reaching for another weapon. Considine shot Meredith three times, once in the chest, once in the heart, and another time in the neck, killing him instantly. John then brushed himself off and handed his gun to Sheriff Cudihee while surrendering. All of this action lasted about ninety seconds.

July 1911—Seattle police officer Henry L. Harris is shot in the back of the head while standing post at the California Tavern on Washington Street and Occidental Avenue. Before he fell to the ground, he was able to fire two shots of his own. But the assailant was believed to have avoided any hit. No one was ever arrested, and the case went unsolved.

Does the city of Seattle still play out theses tragic events, like a silent movie projected on its cold, wet streets? It is possible that these tragic events from the city's past could be haunting our present. As you wander at night through Seattle keep in mind you may be holding a one-time movie pass to a rare showing of the city's violent past.

DOC MAYNARD'S PUBLIC HOUSE

610 First Avenue

David "Doc" Swinson Maynard is well known for his part in making Seattle what it is today. In fact, he is credited as the "Man who invented Seattle."

During his time in Seattle, Doc was a vivacious and generous man who loved his liquor. He also gave away cash or land to just about anyone with a promising idea. After all his generosity, he died essentially landless and broke. The rather revealing epitaph on the tombstone of his second wife, Catherine, reads, "She did what she could." There is a story that the caretakers must reset his stone marker now and again, as it has a habit of slipping into a tipsy position—just like Doc in his lifetime.

Doc Maynard's Public House is a restored 1890s saloon with a gorgeous

DOC MAYNARD'S PUBLIC HOUSE

carved bar that was shipped from Chicago. Rich with history, the pub is one of the oldest buildings in the city. Doc's is located in the heart of Pioneer Square and also serves as the meeting place for the world-famous Seattle Underground Tours.

Folks say that they have heard people walking around when no one was in the area. In one account, an employee was in one of the stalls in the women's restroom, when she heard what she guessed was a co-worker walk in and proceed to the other stall. The employee called but got no response. When she finished, she was surprised to find no one else in the restroom with her. Others have reported seeing a shadowy figure walking around on the upstairs balcony.

While working in the kitchen, one employee would feel a cold spot behind him, and he would also see utensils on the wall swing on their own. One day the activity became so intense with loud banging that he had to turn the volume on the radio up just to ignore the loud sounds.

THE UNDERGROUND TOUR
608 First Avenue

When it came to Seattle rebuilding itself after the Great Seattle Fire of 1889, the new plans helped to develop the underground we tour today. When people from all over the world come to Seattle to visit the Underground, their first impression is, "Oh my, I just paid $15 to see a building's basement." But there really is more to the story than meets the eye.

The city needed to rise above its major drainage problems with its flooding streets and exploding "crappers." Since the city was built at sea level, they knew the first step would be to raise the foundation of the city. Doing so would involve an eight-to-ten year project, and business owners couldn't wait that long to start building their shops. With conflicts of interest, the inhabitants of Seattle had a divided city. Business owners began to build at sea level, while the city fathers built raised streets around their business. Sound complicated? It sure was, and it became much more troublesome when eight-to-thirty-five-feet-high walls surrounded the shops. These walls were then filled in with dirt, rubble from the fire, animal remains, and anything else the builders could find to level the streets off at the top. Seattle had high streets with shops and sidewalks still at sea level! Well, this had to be fixed if for no other reason than to prevent the many deaths from residents falling off the streets onto the sidewalks far below. More than seventeen had already suffered such a fate. After about two years of employing a ladder system at all major intersections to allow shoppers to climb out of one block and down into another, it was time for the sidewalks to be raised to the street level. What was once the second floor would now become the first floor for businesses, and the first floor was now demoted to the basement. This created a tunnel system of underground sidewalks, and the project took twenty years to complete.

It wasn't until 1965 when a local journalist named Bill Speidel was asked about rumors of an Underground Seattle. Curious himself, he discovered the truth of the city's history and started the city's first tours of its underbelly. At that time the underground sections where filled in with trash and castaways from the businesses above. Through the years, Speidel cleaned it up and made the Underground into a fun and entertaining tour for visitors to learn how ridiculous our founders could be.

So now people will see areas that have not been touched since the Underground was condemned, due to plague scares in 1907. Visitors to the Underground can experience smells of dampness and mold, see old business signs, rusted out junk, decay, and a few rats scurrying around.

Korn: The original Korn building was completed just before the Great Seattle Fire, which then destroyed it. Soon after the fire, another building of the same design was put up in its place. Here you will see the old bar from the supply shop that once ran

SEATTLE UNDERGROUND

from this location. Tour guides have reported seeing a shadowy figure leaving the area just as they enter the room. Some say they can even feel a heaviness when entering the room.

Oriental Hotel: This was once a popular hosting spot to the ladies working the streets—also known in Seattle as "the seamstresses." Tourists have seen the glimmering outline of women walking along the old sidewalks. Women on the tours say they can feel their depression. On one late night, ghost investigators experienced strange sounds. In response they asked, "If that's you, please give us a better sign." Right after that, there was a very loud bang that startled everyone present. Right afterwards, an investigator asked, "Was that you?" When it came time to review the recordings, it was discovered that a voice replies in response to the question, "I kicked the can!" Oddly enough, the sound that was heard by the witnesses was that of a garbage can being kicked.

Schwabacher's Basement: Built in 1892 as a hardware company, this site had been used for many things, but at some time in the 70s it was used as a homeless camp, providing shelter on those cold and wet nights for the homeless of Seattle. In the far back corner is a bathroom, and it is believed that a homeless man was killed back there. Some say they have seen him walking around in the basement area. Others can feel him standing above them. Ghost investigators have captured a cloudy substance, known as ectoplasm. Odd noises can be heard, noises that will respond when questions are asked. Also, the sound of children singing has been picked up on recorders. Some tourists have even reported seeing a child in blue jeans and a T-shirt standing alone in the underground.

The Vault: Here, just a few feet away from the popular purple glass skylight, you will see a wooden sign that hangs over a bank teller's cage. For years, this location has been documented in media around the world as one of Seattle's most haunted sites, and it may very well be true.

Story has it that during the gold rush, miners were returning to Seattle with gold in their possession. As more and more gold started to come to Seattle, the town became a more violent city. People would do whatever they could to get hold of the gold. So banks like the Scandinavian-American Bank that once stood here offered a late-night drop-off service. A miner could get his gold to safety even if he missed regular banking hours. This service allowed the bank to convert its underground section into an outside vault.

It is believed that during some of the robberies (and many happened around this time), the teller on duty was killed, along with the miner who was jumped and stabbed to death for his gold. Tour guides and tourists have seen these two dead men in the vault area on many occasions. One story goes that a tour guide in the 1980s ran into the suspected apparition of the bank teller. She described seeing a tall man in a white dress shirt with thick cuff and collar. He was also sporting black suspenders and a handlebar mustache. Not common attire for the 1980s. On one investigation, when asked, "What is your name?" a response was captured on tape saying "Edward." The interesting thing is, on a different investigation with a different group, they also captured a similar recording. When asked the same question, they received the reply: "Eddy." Could one of the gentlemen haunting this spot be named Edward?

Old Theater: This location, which is no longer part of the underground tour but serves as a warehouse for Utilikilts (a kilt shop in Pioneer Square), was once a burlesque theater. While filming a show for Discovery Channel's *America's Ghost Hunters*, local ghost hunters (AGHOST) discovered a very negative presence here. In fact, psychics and sensitives would not venture into the room. Surveillance equipment was set up to monitor during a two-hour period. There was a motion-sensitive camera, a tape recorder, and Scrabble tiles in case any spirits wanted to make contact. This was all done in a controlled environment, which meant all doors were locked. Two hours later, when reentering the locked room, the camera went off, taking the investigators' picture. The investigators then made their way across the room to find that Scrabble tiles had been moved. Three were moved to the top, which spelled C, A, T. The recorder and film were reviewed to find that during the surveillance, the audio recorder picked up what sounded like someone walking up to the recorder, then nothing. The film showed that the camera was working correctly due to the fact that only two pictures appeared: one was the test shot when setting up the camera; the other was the group entering the room at the end of two hours. This shows no one could have entered the room without their knowing it, at least no one of the living sort.

Public Baths: Lots of local hotels didn't offer baths in the room, so public baths became popular for those who wanted to keep clean. It cost twenty-five cents for a nice hot bath to be drawn and half if you came in after 2 p.m. when they recycled the water. Connected to the baths is the Underground gift shop where employees have seen a figure in the window that looks out into the Underground. Books have flown from selves and toilets have flushed on their own. On an investigation, a recording was captured that stated, "Turn on the fan." At that time, the investigators had turned off a fan to produce a more quiet and controlled investigation. They didn't know there was someone of another world who wanted it on.

ARCTIC CLUB
700 Third Avenue

In 1916 veterans of the Yukon Gold Rush decided to come together and form a gentlemen's club called "The Arctic Club." The members commissioned to have their personal headquarters, designed by Seattle architect A. Warren Gould, known as the Arctic Building. This eight-story structure, which features twenty-seven walrus heads adorning the third floor, was completed in 1917. However, the original walrus-tusked ivories were replaced with plastic for fear of skewering pedestrians below. The club's elegant interior included a ladies' tearoom, private dining rooms, billiard and card rooms, a bowling alley, barber shop, and private roof garden. Plus, the Dome Room topped by a Rococo gilt-and-stained-glass skylight remains one of the grandest interiors in downtown Seattle. You may be familiar with the Dome Room if you happen to have seen the Stephen King movie *Rose Red*, as it was featured as the library in the film.

In 1971, the club disbanded and the building was sold to the city of Seattle in 1988. However, as early as 1921 the Arctic Club leased office space to the city, and in 2006 it was purchased by Arctic Club Hotel LLC, restored to its amazing beauty, and reopened in 2008. Now it's a luxurious 120-room hotel operated by the Double Tree. This historic treasure carries a tragic past that may never leave and is still talked about today.

On August 8, 1936, Washington Democratic representative Marion A. Zioncheck fell to his death from this building. Zioncheck's life was a very colorful one prior to its sudden ending. He was born December 5, 1901 in Poland, only to be relocated to Seattle four years later. He was the son of poor immigrants who resided

ARCTIC CLUB

in the Beacon Hill neighborhood. He started out taking on many odd jobs, such as a logger, a cowboy, and even sold rat pelts on a bounty during the plague scares in which rats were targeted as carriers. These and the other twenty odd jobs helped him and his family get by before he was of age to graduate from high school. Later he struggled to complete his schooling that led him to a law degree from the University of Washington.

Marion was indeed a radical, a charmer, and a fighter. He was the first public defender for the dispossessed and the homeless. He had Seattle mayor Frank Edwards recalled in 1931, and he was the first to represent Washington's congressional district as a Democrat.

It was during the Great Depression that Zioncheck was elected to Congress at the age of thirty-two and served from March 4, 1933 until his death. While in office, he was making headlines mostly for extracurricular antics and drunken escapades with his new wife Rubeye Louise Nix, whom he married within a week a one-night stand. One late-night frolic in the Rockefeller Center fountain led to an arrest. He even drove down the sidewalk and then parked on the White House lawn. He was also known to sneak into hotels and hijack the telephone switchboard to wish guests a Happy New Year. At one time, after he had received an eviction notice from his DC apartment, he refused to leave and forcibly dragged his elderly landlady out of her building. Once he himself was tossed out of a formal dinner party for lapping up his soup like a dog. He was known to start and even get involved in student riots and even fights. He and his wife were caught throwing coconuts at people from their hotel window in Puerto Rico while on honeymoon. Some may have found him an interesting character, but others believed he had sanity issues. In fact, he was committed at Gallinger Hospital in DC, but later escaped on Independence Day in 1936.

Due to his unappealing public image, bizarre political events, and recent hospital escape, he was urged

MARION ZIONCHECK

to not run for reelection. Refusing to step down, he came back to Seattle to avoid arrests and began his independent, nonparty-supported reelection campaign. It was at the Arctic Building, that Zioncheck turned the fifth and sixth floors into his campaign headquarters. On August 1 Marion learned that his good friend and co-worker, Warren G. Magnuson, was running against him. This and a rumor that incriminating evidence would become public knowledge if he did not step down may have led to his last days.

On that fateful day of August 7, he completed his will and a farewell note declaring: "*My only hope in life was to improve the condition of an unfair economic system that held no promise to those that all the wealth of even a decent chance to survive let alone live.*" Marion then told his brother-in-law that he was going to grab his jacket and stepped back into his office. Moments later, waiting near the car on the street below, his brother-in-law watched in horror as Zioncheck fell from the window of his fifth-floor office. His body struck the pavement on Third Avenue directly in front of the entrance of the Arctic Club and just outside of the car occupied by his wife. Here, his body remained for several hours until a coroner could be called to assess the situation.

To this day, members of Zioncheck's family believe that he was murdered—pushed out the window—and that the note left behind was not written by him. A private investigator who studied body positions of people who jumped from high places versus those that were pushed concluded that Zioncheck was pushed. Zioncheck had several run-ins with FBI Director J. Edgar Hoover; once Zioncheck had a truckload of manure dumped on Hoover's front steps. Some believed that Hoover was indirectly responsible for Zioncheck's death. Whether it was suicide or murder, many believe Marion is still around for some reason or another.

Folks staying at the Arctic Club have witnessed their share of the bizarre. It seems there are plenty of ghost stories to keep any ghost enthusiast entertained for the night.

The Fourth Floor: Here, guest and employees have described hearing a phantom whistler. These harmonic sounds echo through the halls in the south end. Most times it can be heard in the Nutcracker Suite when no one is around. It is also here that some have felt chills or cold spots.

The Fifth Floor: During the early 1970's there were reports of people hearing ghostly footsteps, the sounds of breathing, and even feeling his presence. This kept the west-end offices vacant for a long time. At one time the police department had offices on the fifth and the sixth floors, and staff would hear what sounded like someone in the office with them, but to their surprise they were utterly alone. The interesting thing is that these reoccurring events always took place near the desk by the window from which Marion had jumped.

What was once his office is now divided into rooms for overnight guests. Be sure to check out rooms 509, 511, 513, 517, and 519. Room 517 is the room from which Zioncheck jumped. Within these rooms some have heard the haunting footsteps of someone pacing back and forth at the foot of the bed, along with feeling an icy breeze. Zioncheck's apparition has been seen roaming about on the fifth floor as well.

The Sixth Floor: In 1996 the Civil Service Commission occupied this floor. It was near the thirtieth anniversary of Marion's death when one of the senior staff had a night she'll never forget. It all started when she was doing some late-night work alone in the building at around 8 p.m. She was greeted by an empty elevator that stopped for no reason on the fifth floor, as if someone were getting off. She then proceeded to the area where she was running copies of reports to be ready for the next morning's meeting. While she ran from room to room, she would leave the lights on to guide her way through the dark halls, only to find when she returned the lights would be shut off. Thinking at first it might just be the security guard working the building, she continued to turn lights back on, only again to find them off when she came back. These events continued throughout the night until she was ready to leave. As she approached the elevators, again to her surprise, before touching the call button, the doors opened to reveal an empty elevator. Was Marion being the gentleman by assisting her for the night?

Events similar to this had been reported for years prior to her encounter. Many had seen lights go off and on by themselves and had heard the sounds of muffled talking only to discover they are completely alone.

The Elevators: Many believe that Marion likes to play with the elevators. Here employees and guests find the elevators are constantly called to the fifth floor for no reason. The doors will open and close on their own to reveal no living presence inside. One woman felt him in the elevator with her as she descended alone to the lobby. Another claims to have seen his ghostly figure in the reflection of the mirrors inside. Other stories talk about feeling a chilling breeze escape the elevators when the doors open. Some say don't be surprised if you happen to ride the elevator down from the upper floors to find it stop on the fifth floor for no apparent reason.

Outside: If you happen to walk by the building on Third Avenue, you may pause to feel a cold spot on the location where his body landed just outside of the hotel's entrance. You may even get the chills, feel a heaviness, or even get dizzy.

Zioncheck may have been forgotten from political and Seattle history, but for the Arctic Club, he still lives on (at least in a spiritual form). Maybe this is his way of leaving his mark in Seattle. One thing we can't deny—Marion Zioncheck had a great run.

See also: *University of Washington* in The University District

Evergreen-Washelli Cemetery in Seattle Cemeteries

MOTHER DAMNABLE

Southwest corner of First and Jackson Streets

Here was where Seattle's first hotel once stood. Named the Felker House, it was run by Mary Ann Conklin, more likely to be known as "Mother Damnable." Conklin received this name due to her fiery temper and profane vocabulary that was equally colorful in French, Spanish, Chinese, Portuguese, and German. Born Mary Ann Boyer in 1821, she married a Russian sea captain of a whaling ship, David W. "Bull" Conklin, in 1851. In 1853 he abandoned her in Port Townsend, Washington, as he sailed off to Alaska. She made her way to Seattle and took up shop with Captain Leonard Felker and ran his local hotel. Eventually, the second floor of the hotel was turned into a well-known brothel run by Mother herself. When the Battle of Seattle approached, Navy military wanted to improve Seattle's defenses by building a road that would pass by the hotel. This threatened the huge bushes surrounding the hotel that secured the discretion of her well-to-do customers. According to memoirs of Thomas Stowell Phelps, the navigator of the U.S. *Decatur*:

> . . . the moment our men appeared upon the scene, with three dogs at her heels, and an apron filled with rocks, this termagant would come tearing from the house, and the way stones, oaths, and curses flew was something fearful to contemplate, and, charging like a fury, with the dogs wild to flash their teeth in the detested invaders, the division invariably gave way before the storm, fleeing, officers and all, as if old Satan himself was after them.

Mother Damnable died in 1873, but her stubbornness still carried on even after death. Her remains where buried in the Seattle Cemetery, later converted into Denny Park in 1884. Her body was then moved to Volunteer Park and then once again to

SCHWABACHER HARDWARE

Lake View Cemetery on Capitol Hill. The workers were surprised it took half a dozen men to lift her coffin from the ground. Her coffin weighed close to thirteen hundred pounds. Curious about the weight, they opened the coffin and found her body had calcified, turned to stone with all details still remaining, even the wickedest smirk on her face. Once word spread about Mother Damnable's condition, PT Barnum of Barnum & Bailey Circus fame, offered a great sum of money to obtain the remains of Mother Damnable for his famous sideshows of freaks. However the city of Seattle refused to part with her body and placed the hardened corpse back into the Seattle soil. It is also believed that maybe her body wasn't moved at all, and she may still be resting somewhere in the heart of downtown Seattle.

Today, on the corner of First and Jackson stands the last of the Schwabacher Hardware buildings, which replaced the Felker House that burned down in the Great Seattle Fire of 1889, built in 1905 and designed by Bebb and Mendel of the Frye Hotel fame. It seems Mother Damnable hasn't let go of her property just yet. Folks in the building have reported hearing curse words whispered into their ears. When they turn to see who's responsible for the profanity, they are surprised to see no one around. In fact, some of these whispered vulgarites were not understood until later translated. Others have seen the frail woman wandering the grounds, while some have had small rocks thrown at them from out of nowhere. So outsiders beware if you venture too close to her property, you may have to battle the wrath of Mother Damnable.

See also: Battle of Seattle in this section

MERCHANTS CAFE

109 Yesler Way

Constructed in 1890, the Merchants Café still has its rustic look. Designed by W. E. Boone (a direct descendent of Daniel Boone), this café is one of the oldest restaurants in Seattle. It started as a saloon when it opened its doors and served five-cent beers to miners waiting their turns at the upstairs brothel. During Prohibition the café survived by converting to a restaurant, while other saloons and taverns closed down.

At times the employees would experience the water turning on and off without assistance. Doors would open and close on their own, glasses would break and objects would move. One night, a bartender had everything shut down and turned to see a woman sitting at the end of the bar. He called out to her and told her the bar was closed and she needed to leave. She just turned to him and smiled. He then thought he was going to have to personally escort her out, but as he approached her, she just vanished before his eyes.

Its top floors were set up as office space; it wasn't until the 1920s when it was used as the Merchants Hotel. In service until the 1930s, the former hotel is now an apartment building. A few employees of the café have lived upstairs and have had unseen visitors. One young female employee was staying on the third floor, and she

MERCHANT'S CAFÉ

would sometimes feel someone crawl in bed with her and place unseen hands on her stomach as if to hold her down. Another employee saw a man in a top hat walk by his bathroom door as he was brushing his teeth.

If you get a chance you might want to venture to the basement. Here is where a frightened cook ran upstairs to let the rest of the employees know something threw an ice scoop at him. He then refused to go back downstairs. So whether you would like to peek at its ghosts or just its history, you need to make a stop here.

OK HOTEL

212 Alaskan Way S

This place was once known as the OK or the Old Klondike Hotel. Locals called it the OK Hotel because it was an OK place to hang out. In the 1990s it was a bar and music club but closed in 2001 due to damages from the Nisqually earthquake. Before the earthquake, local bands played here, including Nirvana. Its heyday was during the prime of the gold rush when miners were heading to Seattle to strike it rich. At that time, this hotel offered twenty-five rooms and one bathroom on each floor. Most eight-by-nine-foot rooms would comfortably sleep one person, and, normally, four or five men would share the room, sleeping in shifts. It now is an affordable housing apartment building with an art gallery in the lobby.

OK HOTEL

People had reported strange events taking place here—they have seen apparitions forming and have felt as though they were being touched when no one is around. In one report, a couple visiting the site was startled to see an older couple descend the staircase only to vanish when they reached the bottom. One of the owners had an apartment on the second floor and would wake in the middle of the night to the sounds of someone whistling in the bar below. Startled by this, he would race down to find no living person in sight. Employees have felt the temperatures drop suddenly, hear doors open and then close when no one is around, and they've heard creepy sounds throughout the night.

STAR BAR

309 First Avenue S

Once known as Wild Palm Bar and Grill, this place has not been the friendliest to any new owners. The spirits haunting this site have made things difficult for most who

STAR BAR

work here. Employees have heard what sounds like someone running across the upstairs balcony, but when they go to investigate, no one is there. Glasses have exploded or been thrown across the room by unseen forces. Strange noises and smells have been reported. But most odd, the employees found writing in ketchup on the ceiling of the bar that appeared to be a giant letter "V."

It seems that this location has had problems with business owners constantly running out—whether it is due to financial troubles or spirits running amuck. No one seems to be able to handle what this location has to offer. As of now it is home to a new club called Aura, and maybe by the time you read this book it could be a whole new venue. Whatever haunts this site, most don't like the feeling they get when they are alone here. Could this be the work of a very unhappy entity not willing to share its environment with the living?

THE SMITH TOWER
506 Second Avenue

This forty-two-story building is the oldest skyscraper in Seattle. Started in 1912 and completed in 1914, it is named after its builder, Lyman Cornelius Smith of Smith & Corona typewriters. When completed, it held the record as being the tallest building west of the Mississippi River until 1931. But the building still held the record on the West Coast until the Space Needle surpassed it in 1962. It is also one of the last buildings on the West Coast to have hand-operated elevators.

The thirty-fifth floor of the tower is home to The Chinese Room, which is also the observatory deck. The room is finely decorated

THE SMITH TOWER

with gifts of furniture and a hand-carved ceiling from the Empress of China. This also includes the famous Wishing Chair. Legend has it that if an unmarried woman who wants to be married sits in this chair, she will be married within a year. The legend came true for Smith's daughter, who married in the Chinese Room herself a year after visiting the tower.

Security guards have experienced odd things happening throughout the night while standing watch over the building. The old elevators would be called to floors when no one is in the building. Noises of doors closing and things moving have been heard on empty floors. While watching the security monitors, they have seen shadowy figures appear on the screens. They have also reported having sudden cold breezes fly by them when doing their rounds. Other employees have seen a woman roaming the Chinese Room. She will walk into rooms and never be seen again, sometimes vanishing in front of their eyes. The ghost is believed to be the daughter of L.C. Smith himself. At one time there was an exhibit honoring Bertha Landes, Seattle's first female mayor. While the event was going on, many claimed to see her spirit overlooking the exhibit.

See also: Harvard Exit Theatre in Capitol Hill

PIONEER SQUARE HOTEL
77 Yesler Way

This historic landmark started out as the Hotel Yesler of Henry Yesler fame. Completed in 1914, it was not until the mid-1990s that the Best Western chain bought the hotel. They restored the building and opened it as The Pioneer Square Hotel, currently the only hotel in the Pioneer Square Historic District. Stories have it that after the hotel fell on hard times and became inhabited by prostitutes and other lower-class citizens during the 1970s, the building was transformed into a "flophouse." At this time, one of the owners made agreements with some of the homeless to collect their social security checks in exchange for permanent residency in the hotel. Little did people know that if transients died while in his care, he neglected to report the deaths and continued to collect their checks. How he got away with this crime for some time was that he hid these deaths by burying the bodies in the basement of the hotel.

Employees say they don't like to be alone in the basement. Many have heard odd noises, seen a dark figure lurking about, and have watched objects move without

PIONEER SQUARE HOTEL

assistance. One employee stated that while alone in the basement a box slid across the floor all on its own. In addition to the weird happenings in the basement, maids have reported that TVs will turn on and off on their own. In fact, guests have had to unplug TVs because they will continue to act up throughout the night by turning on and switching channels.

One guest returns every year and checks into the same room every time, claiming it's haunted by a little girl. They say the guest enjoys the ghost who combs the guest's long hair throughout the night. Other guests have felt what feels like a medium-sized dog crawl on to the beds. One couple reported feeling what they described to be energy passing through their room, followed by whispering voices throughout the night.

If you enjoy sharing your room with unseen guests, this might be the place for you. Many ghost hunters have stayed here and have picked up voices on their recorders. So if you do try a night or two here, make sure you come prepared.

THE ROCKY MOUNTAIN CHOCOLATE FACTORY

99 Yesler Avenue

The Rocky Mountain Chocolate Factory now resides in what was once the Scandinavian-American Bank in the old Yesler Building built in 1891. It stands

CHOCOLATE FACTORY

over the very spot of the underground vault that is one of the most documented sites of haunted Seattle, and has a storage area right next to the old vault.

Employees of The Rocky Mountain Chocolate Factory and past workers from former businesses on the location have reported strange activity happening in the lower basement area, including sightings of an old-time miner walking around and vanishing once someone makes eye contact with him. One manager, while working alone in the basement, had the feeling of someone standing behind him when no one is around. One time he actually felt a hand on his shoulder, which caused him to immediately pick up his papers and leave for the night.

They also say things will be moved around after clearly being placed somewhere else. Very loud noises can also be heard coming from the basement. When investigated, there is no sign of any disturbances. Could the man seen haunting the vault area be the same man in the basement of The Rocky Mountain Chocolate Factory?

See also: Underground Tour (The Vault) in this Section

MUTUAL LIFE BUILDING

605 First Avenue

First called the Yesler Building, the name was changed when Mutual Life Insurance Company of New York bought the building in 1897. On September 10, 1985, an Asian art performance company came to Seattle to perform a very rare piece known as Sankai Juku. Here the artists dressed completely in white and covered their entire bodies with white rice paint, appearing as ghostly apparitions. These four dancers were then suspended by their ankles from the top of the building and slowly lowered as they twisted and moved in sync with one another. Once the artists started to descend, a rope snapped and the second-from-the-left performer plummeted six floors to his death. This tragedy was witnessed by the hundreds of onlookers, who saw his body in a fetal position on the corner of First and Yesler. Eerily and coincidentally, the performance piece was called "The Dance of Birth and Death." It was also discovered that the performers had purchased used rope from a local shipyard as it allowed

MUTUAL LIFE BUILDING

them to move more freely because new rope is too tight. The sad thing is that they only tested three of the ropes before the performance. It was the fourth one that took the young man's life. Analyzing the offending rope, it was discovered with laboratory analysis that the rope was degraded by a chemical that had come into contact with it before it was purchased.

Today, around the tenth of every September, people see a ghostly white figure twisting and floating above the building. This apparition will last for about fifteen seconds and then just fade into the sky. It is strongly believed the artist wants to complete his last dance.

DENUNZIO'S RESTAURANT

102 Cherry Street

This location served as a speakeasy, a dime-a-dance hall, a skid row theater, and was used as storage space just before Luigi DeNunzio purchased it in 1989 and turned it into the underground Italian gem it is today. This restaurant features authentic tastes of European cuisine, but it also serves up a healthy portion of ghost stories.

A few employees have seen shadowy figures roaming around. One evening, a few workers were hanging out after closing when they heard what sounded like dishes

DENUNZIO'S

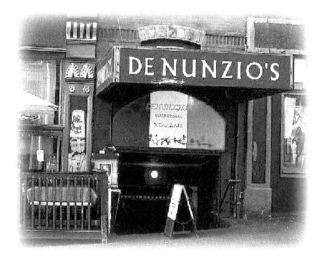

clanging together. They went to investigate and found two espresso cups sitting empty on an unused table and still warm to the touch. No one had any clue as to how the cups arrived on this table.

One person saw a little girl run up the stairs only to vanish halfway up the flight. There are also reports of a woman appearing in the ladies' restroom. Perhaps both stories feature remnants of a historic underground past. Most people feel there is something hanging out here, and in 2009 they had AGHOST investigate. During the investigation, the team discovered unexplained EMF readings and a recording of a voice. When asked, "Can you hear me?" the voice replied, "I can hear you."

Unfortunately, DeNunzio's has closed its doors for good, leaving its ghosts behind for a new owner to encounter lurking in the shadows.

MYSTERY BOOKSHOP
117 Cherry Street

For those who love a good mystery novel, this place can be a dream come true. But the biggest mystery may be the one experienced by one of its employees. When the shop opened in 1990 in an underground location of the Broderick Building at 113 Cherry Street, the staff was unaware that their little bookshop carried more than just books. One employee was working alone when she saw a man in a long jacket and black hat walk by. When she went to address the customer, he disappeared behind the shelves of books never to be seen again. This was not the only time she saw this gentlemen. She saw him from time to time, and she became accustomed to his presence. It wasn't until months later, when another man came into the store with more interest in the shop than its books, that things fell into place. The curious shopper told her that his great grandfather ran a barber shop in this very spot, many years ago. He then proceeded to pull out a picture of his grandfather that showed a man in a long trench coat and black bowler hat. To her shock, this was a photo of the same man she saw haunting the shop.

In 2005, the Mystery Book Shop moved just down the hall, but they still keep a watchful eye out for their ghostly friend next door.

See also: Broderick Building in this section

UNITED WAY BUILDING
720 Second Avenue

In 2003 United Way took over the old Seattle National Bank, built in 1921. Prior to that, a small church and cemetery once stood on this property. The twenty-four-by-forty foot "Little White Church," as it was named due to its white paint, was built in 1855, making it Seattle's first house of worship. Along with it came the city's first formal cemetery as well. The first documented burials in the Little White Church Cemetery rest on the southwest corner of Second Avenue and Columbia Street, right next to the church, and were the final resting places of two young men killed in the Battle of Seattle in 1856. Other burials included Jonathan Denny, the infant son of David and Louisa Denny, who died in 1867 only a few hours old. The burials in the church cemetery were eventually removed and transported to the Seattle Cemetery.

UNITED WAY BUILDING

The Little White Church existed for ten years before it closed. The church building reopened and served as many different things besides a church; it also was a gambling hall, a saloon, a restaurant, and a vaudeville house, until it burned down in the Great Seattle Fire of 1889.

Today, working in the United Way building offers a more unique experience for its employees. Workers have seen apparitions wandering through the halls, heard talking when no one is around, and have also reported dark figures streaking by.

One night a few volunteers where working late stuffing gift bags. They noticed loud noises of things being moved around upstairs, thinking it may be a co-worker. To their surprise, they discovered they were the only ones left in the building.

When United Way took over the building, they had a night custodian who quit after she would see a man frequently approach her and then disappear. She described him as a tall, slender man from the early 1900s, maybe slightly before. What scared her the most was his face, which she said looked scarred, as if he had been burned.

Could the activity reported here be the result of building a structure over what was once a cemetery? Could the man seen here be a survivor from the Great Seattle Fire? Whatever it might be, these spirits may be looking at how times have changed or may be trapped in a time forgotten.

See also: Denny Park in Belltown; Battle of Seattle in this section

FRYE'S HOTEL

FRYE'S HOTEL

101 Third Avenue S

Built in 1911 by George Frye, this was once labeled Seattle's finest hotel but is now called the Hotel of Death. Converted to low-income housing in the 1970s, this hotel has had its share of bad luck. In 2006, when twenty-nine homicides were reported in downtown Seattle, this hotel accounted for 20 percent of them in six months alone.

A woman jumped from the ninth floor, after claiming unknown forces were out to get her. A man and woman were found dead on the kitchen floor of their apartment. A woman was stabbed to death by her neighbor when he accused her of stealing his keys. Many suicides and overdoses have also plagued this site. But the tragedies are not all recent—George Frye died the same year this building was completed.

Residents have complained about hearing a woman scream late into the night. Doors and windows will open and close on their own. Dark figures have been seen roaming the halls, and horrendous smells appear form nowhere. As to what deadly forces might be at play, who knows? But I would not suggest taking up residency here unless you like to play with the dead.

TEMPLE BILLIARDS

126 South Jackson Street

Pool and spirits—the bottled kind— are what people come here for. But, at times, visitors might get more than they bargained for. Employees have had strange things happen beyond the run-of-the-mill drunken partying. They say that when things are quiet, after closing or before opening, odd noises can be heard. Shadowy figures have been seen in the basement. One time after closing, a bartender was looking in the mirror and saw a guy run by and go into the restroom. When the employee went to investigate and remove the stranger from the bar, he was surprised to find no one there. Many say they never feel alone here, even when no one is around.

TEMPLE BILLIARDS

JOSEPH AND THE
CHUCKHOLE
Third Avenue and Jackson Street

Late one night, Barbara was driving home around 10 p.m. after a company Christmas party. It was a clear night when she passed Second Avenue on Jackson Street. Right after that she suddenly slammed on her brakes as a small boy stood in the path of her car. Clearly she thought she had run over the child. Shocked and in a panic, she quickly jumped out of the car while fussing with her cell phone to call 911. While she was doing this, she proceeded to look around for the injured boy, but there was no sign of him until she realized his body must be still under her car. At this point, an older man came over to assist her. Afraid to see the condition of the child, she asked with tears in her eyes if the man look under her car for the body. He proceeded to do so, but there was no child in sight. They both looked around the area but found no child.

In the 1800s Seattle suffered from drainage problems, due to being built at sea level. Tidal waters would flood city streets. The rain and plumbing problems didn't help. With the streets being used by horses and wagons, they developed huge potholes, also known as chuckholes, throughout the downtown streets. These chuckholes where so bad that they refilled them with sawdust, which only made matters worse. The mixture of water, soil, and sawdust became a substance similar to quicksand in most areas. To avoid running into these ever-growing obstructions throughout the Seattle streets, the city decided to put them on city maps to guide citizens through the streets more safely.

In 1898 a ten-year-old boy named Joseph Bufonchio was playing at the corner of Third and Jackson in what was known as the Great Jackson Street Chuckhole—it was eight feet deep and sixteen feet wide. The local children loved to play in these large pools of muck. These children would build rafts and push themselves across these miniature lakes by using poles to push them along. In doing so, Joseph's pole got stuck at the bottom of the chuckhole, and he fell in and sank. It took the locals hours before they where able to retrieve his body at the bottom.

After that tragic event, newspapers read, "Boy Drowned in Seattle Streets." Embarrassed by the incident, the city of Seattle made rules to prevent anyone else from drowning by placing life preservers at all intersections and demanding that all children learn to swim. Could the young boy seen on Third and Jackson be the downed boy, Joseph? Keep an eye out and see.

PIONEER BUILDING
600 First Avenue

Completed in 1891 on the same property that Henry Yesler's house once stood, this six-floor building originally had a seventh-floor tower room (with a pyramidal roof) that was removed because of damage from the 1949 earthquake. Today the building is filled with offices. During the Klondike Gold Rush of 1897, at least forty-eight different mining firms had offices in this building.

Workers and guests have seen the figure of an older, gray-haired man walking around the various floors of the building, peeking into offices. He has also been heard walking up and down the halls on the creaky floors when no one is in sight. People have suggested that this man may be Henry Yesler himself.

PIONEER BUILDING

Henry Yesler had had a very interesting long life when he died in 1892 at age eighty-two. It was filled with corruption, fraud, anger, money, and lots of free love. However there is one thing that might lead us to believe that Henry still has claims to the Pioneer Building. It seems that in June of 1859, Henry and his wife, Sarah, had gotten word that their twelve-year-old son whom they had left in the care of family in Ohio had died from an illness. It was at this time that Spiritualism (the practice of commuting with spirits) had become a worldwide phenomenon. So after learning the fate of their son, they turned to the spirit world by conducting séances and seeking the help from mediums across the globe in hopes to make contact with their beloved son.

Could Yesler's better understanding of the spirit world help him to watch over the city he help put on the map? Or is he still in search of his son lost at such a young age?

INTERURBAN BUILDING

102 Occidental Way

Formerly known as the Seattle National Bank Building, it was completed in 1892. The corner entrance, with the carved lion's head, was the bank's main entrance. Back when the gold rush was big in Seattle, many locals were pulling scams to get as much money from the miners as possible before sending them off to Alaska. This was known as "mining the miners." Violet McNeal, also known as "Princess Plum Blossom," "Princess Lotus Blossom," "Princess Flower Blossom," or "Princess Cherry Blossom" was no stranger to this way of life. In fact, she and her husband, Will "Tiger Fat" Davies, ran a bogus clinic known as the Yokohama Medical Clinic from the second floor of this building. It is believed that she would stand on the corner, dressed in Japanese garb, claim to have miracle cures from the Orient, and offer free medical exams to all who crossed her path. After these exams she would sell these cures for illnesses at a very cheap rate. The potions would include strong astringents like spices,

INTERURBAN BUILDING

oils, alcohol, and opium. Once her customers started taking these medicines, they would become addicted to the concoctions and their effects on the human mind. It's when their vials became empty that things took a more interesting turn. When they would return for a new prescription, Violet would be more than happy to refill it, but only at a higher price, making Violet Seattle's first drug dealer.

Many of her patients would also return seeking Violet's help for their addiction to her "cures," where she would administer a treatment known as a Cayenne Enema. No doubt that she would charge a pretty penny for this procedure as well.

Violet also claimed to have access to the medicine that allegedly saved the Chinese race from extinction, called Vital Sparks, which gave males virility and sexual vigor, and would sell it at medicine shows. This "miracle" was actually candy, called buckshot, moistened and rolled in bitter aloe powder and poured into a box.

In 1947, Violet published her autobiography, *Four White Horses and a Brass Band* and retired to Mountain View, California, where she later died.

People walking by this location have seen a ghostly woman in Japanese robes appearing at a second-floor window. She has also been seen wandering the halls on that floor. Some have even seen her standing on the corners near the building. Could this be Violet still looking for new victims for her addictive cures?

MEGAN MARY OLANDER FLORISTS
222 First Avenue S

On the corner of First and Main, you can't miss this sweet little flower shop run by Megan herself. Nestled in the far end corner of what is known as the Grand Central Building, which stands where Squire's Opera House once stood in 1879. During the Great Seattle fire, the Opera House burned down to the ground and was rebuilt as the Squire-Latimer Building, later becoming the lavish Grand Central Hotel.

When the depression of the 1930s hit Seattle, the hotel closed, and the building sat vacant until the 1970s when it took on major renovations and stands as we now see it. So when Megan purchased the shop, she had no idea it came with a ghost. From day one, she would open her shop and discover the radio playing, even though she swore she had turned it off the night before. This then became a regular habit. She also felt

MEGAN'S FLOWERS

cold spots and would hear the door shake when no one was near. One day, a mirror resting against a table started to shake and slowly levitated off the ground. When it reached a few inches up, it suddenly dropped. Surprisingly enough, the mirror didn't break. As to who might be lingering in her shop, no one knows for sure. But stop by and you might be lucky enough to experience something odd for yourself.

Megan Mary Olander Florists has moved, but hopefully the ghost has not. As of 2011 this location remains empty; however, Megan moved her shop to Capitol Hill.

THE CENTRAL

207 First Avenue S

Built in 1892, this structure housed Watson Bros. Famous Restaurant on the first floor and Skagit Hotel on the upper floors. In 1901 the building was sold and renamed The Seattle Bar and operated by Peter Gessner, a well-known gambler. The location was commonly called the Central Tavern or Central Café, later known as Central Saloon, which is what it is still called today.

Many locals may even remember the days when this place used to bring in little-known local bands like Nirvana, Alice in Chains, Soundgarden, and Mudhoney as well as college-station favorites like Sonic Youth and Jane's Addiction in the 1980s.

It's not odd to hear of strange things happening while working in this historic site. At times, employees will hear talking when alone in the bar. There is a camera that watches over the stage during performances. Every so often odd things have been

THE CENTRAL

caught on the monitor like strange lights flashing and even shadowy figures gliding across the screen. There have also been reports of hearing the sounds of walking on the hardwood floors when no one is around. It seems the employees are more curious about who this might be and what will happen next.

Many employees and visitors have witnessed seeing a woman in white with her hair nicely swept up in a bun wandering the saloon and upper floors. It seems that when she is spotted, she will vanish before your eyes. Along with her sightings, others talk about hearing footsteps and doors opening and closing in the upstairs area that was once a hotel and has been renovated into offices. Who are the ghosts haunting this site? Some say it very well could be the women who kept themselves busy entertaining the men of Seattle.

See also: The Georgetown Castle in Georgetown

J & M
CAFE
201 First Avenue S

This three-story, brick building was built in 1889, just months after the Great Seattle Fire. In its day, it had hotel rooms on the upper floors with a bar and card room on the main floor. The card room was popular during the card-playing days from 1906 to 1916, which they called the "Wide Open Days" to describe a time when gambling was tolerated due to the lack of authority in Seattle. J & M went by many different names through the years, including J & M Hotel, J & M Bar & Card Room, and Jamieson & Moffett Saloon (from which the term J & M originated). It was during Prohibition that the establishment changed to J & M Café to keeps its doors open by selling soft drinks and meals.

The bar and card room had been up and running since the Gold Rush

THE J & M CAFÉ

days of 1897, but closed its doors in 2009 for a few months. Unfortunately, most of its historic relics were auctioned off when it closed for the short period of time.

Many employees share the story of a ghost in the basement. Here they would see an apparition standing near an old ticket booth, trying to buy a ticket. The ticket booth had been left behind from the days when the basement was dubbed a movie house during the renovation of Seattle. During the 1980s ghostly footsteps and crashing noises where heard in the upstairs area. For over sixty years, the old rooms of the J & M Hotel that flourished on the upper floors have remained empty and are lifeless to this day. Now there is nothing more than abandoned rooms and decay. Many felt that there were ghosts wandering about. It was at this time a couple went exploring for ghostly inhabitants with a 35mm camera. After encountering a few bumps in the night, they scurried home and discovered an apparition in their pictures. They sold that picture to a local magazine, which published it.

Others have reported glasses moving on their own, lights turning off and on, and many employees and guests have felt as if somebody or something touched them in the bar. If ghosts are taking up residence in Seattle, here is a place they are sure to be found.

MARCUS' MARTINI HEAVEN

88 Yesler Way

MARCUS' MARTINI HEAVEN

Just like all the buildings in Pioneer Square, this was built after the Great Fire of 1889. It opened its doors to the public in 1899. You may want to wander down into its underground surroundings, where it is a dimly lit environment, and where many of the staff have experienced some strange occurrences. There have been reports of objects moving, odd sounds, and even the sighting of a shadowy figure here and there. In fact, one employee after working the closing shift claimed to have had a full-on encounter with the ghost himself. After that, the employee refused to work nights. Could there be ghosts lurking in the bar's darkened corners?

Marcus' Martini Heaven is now closed. As of 2011, Pho Express occupies this location.

DUTCH NED

Corner of First Avenue and Yesler Street

Born Nils Jacob Ohm in 1828, this Dutchman arrived in Seattle in 1854. Nick-named "Dutch Ned" by the locals, he was a funny old man who was a bit slow due to a childhood injury. He made his living filling in the potholes throughout Pioneer Square's streets with sawdust from Yesler's sawmill.

Dutch Ned didn't make much money and lived in a small shack on the corner of Bellevue Avenue and Republican Street. His biggest fear was to be forgotten and left to die in his pitiful shack. So he spent most of his hard-earned money on a beautiful stone-and-marble mausoleum at Lake View Cemetery. Being so proud of this lavish landmark, he would spend most of his spare time reading and hosting picnics from what he called his "Little House."

DUTCH NED'S MAUSOLEUM

In his latter years, many of the locals would tease him by stating that when his time had come, they'd just toss his old bones in Potters Field. Fearing this to be true, the poor old man would spend every spare moment in the parlor of the Bonney-Watson Funeral home, sitting and waiting for God's angels to carry him away.

In death, he was indeed laid to rest in his mausoleum. But his life-long dream would come to a sad end. In the 1970s his "Little House" had to be torn down as it was falling apart. All that remains is a portion of the marble door where his body lays at rest. Or is he at rest?

Some say that Dutch Ned's spirit roams the streets of Pioneer Square. He can be seen standing on a corner in his overalls with his shovel in his hand. But most of all, he is seen wandering the grounds of Lake View Cemetery as well. It is believed that his spirit won't rest until he finds his favorite little spot in the world, his "Little House."

See also: Joseph and the Chuckhole in this Section; Lake View Cemetery in Capitol Hill

THE DOUBLE HEADER
407 Second Avenue

This place has had a colorful history since it opened in 1933. It was just after Prohibition when it was converted from a dance hall to the bar it is today. It got its name because it was the first Seattle bar to have a ladies' room as well as a men's room— this was back when no other taverns would serve women. In the1930s it served as a gay bar, but as Pioneer Square fell into despair by the late 1970s, the gay community

moved to Capitol Hill. It is still a bar, but doesn't focus of a specific clientele. You can still hang out and see what Seattle's oldest gay bar looks like. With black-and-white pictures of drag queens on the wall, you might even find some old glitter imbedded in the hard wood floors.

It seems some of its colorful customers might still be hanging around. They say there's a spot on the old dance floor where you can feel a cold spot. There is also a woman who appears in the mirror. Could this be one of the drag queens wanting to

THE DOUBLE HEADER   perform one last time?

88 KEYS
315 Second Avenue S

Constructed in 1900 and former home to saddle manufacturing company Duncan & Sons until 1976, this is now home to a piano bar, retail offices above, and possibly a few ghosts. It seems this place has had its share of odd events, such as chairs falling over on their own, objects flying from shelves, unexplained images showing up on the monitors, and shadowy figures lurking in corners.

The bar area seems to be flooded with ghostly activity. Here many witnesses have seen glasses topple off the shelves one after the other. This had happened so often that the owner, Dino, replaced all his glassware with plastic. Dino also reports encountering loud knockings on his office door when no one else was reported in the bar. One time, during a performance, he watched as unseen hands pushed a woman who was sitting on top of the piano onto the floor.

The owner walked in one morning after being there late into the night and found the stove burners turned on high. It scared him to think a spirit would turn them on and leave them running all night. He's very grateful the place didn't burn down.

The night custodian has had strange things happen to him. While in the basement, he claims that a Native American ghost told him of a body that is buried under the basement floor. Could this be the work of a man who just wants a proper burial?

BRODERICK BUILDING
623 Second Avenue

Once known as The Bailey Building, this building was built in 1892. A well-to-do real estate owner named Henry Broderick had his offices in this building for forty-three years. In 1986, the building was renamed in his honor. In the early twentieth century, the building was known as the Railway Exchange Building because it housed various railway and steamship companies, also professional offices, and even a popular seer and Spiritualist, Mrs. Pettibone.

BRODERICK BUILDING

It seems that on the fifth floor, there have been reports of a woman walking the halls wearing a Victorian dress. There have also been smells of a rose-like perfume in the air. Most of the time, it is smelled just after getting a quick glimpse of the woman or part of her clothing darting around a corner. One report was that a secretary was at her desk when she looked up to see a woman sitting in the waiting room observing the magazines on the table. Not thinking too much of her style of dress, the secretary turned back to her work, then thought for a second about who she might be waiting for, and then turned back to ask if she could be helped, only to find the woman was gone.

Could this be Mrs. Pettibone, having fun with the folks with whom she shares the floor? Or could this be another woman who has passed and we've forgotten?

See also: The Mystery Bookshop in this section

THE SEATTLE HOTEL
First Avenue and Yesler Street

This location started out as one of Seattle's first hotels, which was built in 1861 and known as the Occidental Hotel. A wooden building, its claim to fame was holding the memorial services for President James Garfield in 1881 after he died from injuries sustained after being shot. In 1883 the building was torn down for a grander hotel of the same name. This hotel lasted until 1889 when it burned in the Great Seattle Fire, which destroyed thirty-three blocks of downtown. The next day, building began for a new hotel but with new rules that all downtown buildings were built of nothing but brick, stone, and iron to help prevent the city from burning down again. This brick triangle building was completed in 1890 and renamed the Seattle Hotel or better known as Hotel Seattle to the locals. The hotel lasted as one of the highlights until 1914 when it was converted into offices.

In 1961 the building was abandoned due to the neighborhood falling into despair. In hopes of reshaping the old Pioneer Square area, the city decided on the development of new garages for the growing traffic in downtown. The hotel was the first to come down for that reason. So in that same year, in its place went a parking structure that locals called the Sinking Ship, because it resembles the bow of a ship sticking out of the street.

Haunting Fact

The topic of talking to ghosts became mainstream when two young girls claimed to have communications with a dead man in 1848.

These young ladies where known as the Fox sisters, and their stories claimed worldwide media attention with a knocking ghost in their upper New York home.

Their attempts at talking to the spirit were as simple as one knock for "Yes" and two knocks for "No."

This is how mediums, people who claim to communicate with the dead, became popular through the hype of what would become known as Spiritualism.

THE SEATTLE HOTEL

Shortly after the construction of the new parking garage, locals fought to preserve the neighborhood for its historic value. In 1970 the battle was won, and Pioneer Square became the Historic District, saving the rest of the buildings within its territory.

The memory of the grand hotel that once stood here still haunts those who pay it a visit. Many people have claimed to see ghostly figures walking on air on unseen floors or passing through invisible doors. Some have heard voices and the sounds of partying with old-time music playing in the background. Could these be memories trapped from a time forgotten of a hotel that may never rest in peace?

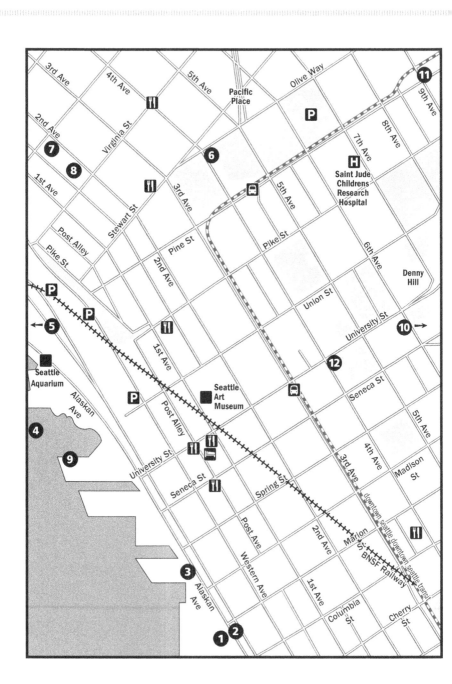

3. WATERFRONT AND DOWNTOWN

Downtown Seattle's Waterfront is the largest little neighborhood on the West Coast. Metropolitan Tract is near the center of downtown. Owned by the University of Washington, this area was the former location of the university's campus. Now this is Seattle's main financial district, waterfront, and shopping areas.

The whole of downtown includes Pike Place Market and Pioneer Square, but the Waterfront area is perhaps the greatest attraction for visitors to the city.

Along the piers are many attractions, including the Seattle Aquarium, cruise terminals, Seattle's Waterfront Arcade, and lots of shopping, including everyone's favorite—Ye Olde Curiosity Shop, which hosts The Spooked In Seattle Tours.

MAP MARKERS

1. Ye Olde Curiosity Shop
2. Ivar's
3. The Haunted Ferry
4. The Sea King
5. Pier 70
6. Mayflower Park Hotel
7. The Crystal Pool
8. Hotel Commodore
9. Carousel
10. Jensonia Hotel
11. Paramount Theatre
12. Fairmount Hotel

GOLD RUSH

In 1897 a steamer ship known as the SS *Portland* docked in Seattle rumored to be carrying a ton of gold. This was not true; it ended up being *two* tons of Alaskan gold, valued at $700,000.

This story brought national media attention to Seattle, and the city officials decided to use this media to help bring more folks to Seattle. So they came up with the idea to start advertising themselves as "The Gateway to Alaska." But Seattle was no gateway to Alaska; in fact, it was almost two thousand miles to the claim sites.

The city's main focus was to make as much money as possible. So this led to many schemes and scams, which the locals called "mining the miners." With thousands of men coming into Seattle hoping to strike it rich, the locals would make sure they got as much money from the miners before sending them on their way to Alaska.

Canada had a lot to do with making Seattle the successful city it is today. With so many miners and explorers crossing its borders and dying before they could make it to Alaska, Canada was often shipping bodies back to the States. This led Canada to pass a law called the "one ton law." Under this law, the only way someone could cross into Canada was if their supplies weighed in at one ton per person. Since Seattle was

GOLD RUSH

While this vision was quite startling to those who witnessed it, some tried to make sense of what they saw. Many of the local tribes buried their dead near the water, and this ghostly walker may very well be near his burial site. If he was buried in this area, it is possible that he was seeking his people. With all of the changes in and around the area, perhaps he was looking to see where his people had gone.

YE OLDE CURIOSITY SHOP
1001 Alaskan Way (Pier 54)

Located on Pier 54, it was founded by J. E. "Daddy" Standley in 1899 and owned by four generations of the same family. Once known as Standley's Free Museum, this unique shop of oddities and strange curiosities brings in tourists from around the world. Many like to see the mummies, the mermaid, shrunken heads, and two-headed animals. But there is far more to see than just these curiosities in this still free-to-gawk shop. Ye Olde Curiosity Shop also features the Spooked In Seattle Tours.

YE OLDE CURIOSITY SHOP

It may have to do with the dead bodies that rest inside or maybe other forces at play, but Ye Olde Curiosity Shop has had some strange events going on. Most of the paranormal activity picked up after they purchased a new location to help expand their overcrowded shop. With another shop just across the way, this allowed them to do some renovations on the old shop. In most cases, when renovations are done to a location, whether it is a home or business, it can stir up paranormal energies. Right away employees were hearing strange noises, seeing things being moved around, things falling off the walls—and a few employees claim to have been touched by unseen hands. But most will agree that they've heard piano music late at night.

An investigation by AGHOST was done on this shop and a psychic brought everyone's attention to an abandoned grand piano in the upstairs storage area. This piano had been abandoned for years and placed up there because the legs had been broken. But, with the aging and neglect, the cords had rusted through and piles of dust had crusted over to the point that no sound would ever emerge from it again. And yet, it emits strange energies, and investigators picked up piano music that was not heard but only recorded on their recorders that night. Could this be the works of a haunted piano?

IVAR AND THE DOCTOR
1001 Alaskan Way (Pier 54)

Ivar Haglund, known today for his chain of Ivar's seafood restaurants, was a very well-known man in Seattle in his day. Born March 21 1905, Haglund came from an old Seattle family. His grandparents had owned Alki Point in 1868 after purchasing it from pioneer Doc Maynard himself. Haglund was raised by his father after his mother, Daisey Maud Haglund, had died from starvation in 1908 when he was just three years old.

The story is that Ivar and his mother had checked into a clinic in Olalla, Washington. The clinic was run by world famous Dr. Linda Hazzard, who was using what she called the fasting cure. Popularity was growing on the idea that fasting could cure most ailments, even cancer. Ivar's mother had suffered from hysteria and it was believed to have been passed on to Ivar himself. Ivar and his mother hoped that the doctor would be able to cure both from this illness.

At a time when most women entered the medical profession as nurses, Dr. Linda Burfield Hazzard had become a well-known qualified physician. She stood up for

IVAR'S

her gender, challenged the medical establishment, and became a leading advocate for natural ways of healing. She had written books such as *Fasting for the Cure of Disease* and had set up shop in the Seattle area by 1907. Back then many folks were being swindled by the latest and greatest miracle.

Since Dr. Hazzard was the first in the United States to receive a degree as a "fasting specialist," people from all over the world would come to her to take part in this new fad of fasting. Here in the small town of Olalla, across the Puget Sound from Seattle, stood the foundation of Dr. Hazzard's madness known as Wilderness Heights. Nestled in complete and utter isolation, her patients would not be allowed to have any contact with the outside world as their bodies shed pound after pound of what was believed to be the purification of the body's "evils" and "toxins." Her patients would live off of small amounts of tomato, orange, and asparagus juice for days, weeks, or even months. She even required daily enemas and provided vigorous massages to accelerate the process. Those of her wealthier patients found the new treatment had left them with empty bellies and empty wallets and had not lived up the promises she had made. Dozens of people would not live to have a healthier life due to her practices and treatment.

Dr. Hazzard had a way to "encourage" her patients to hand over or sign over valuable property, and she's believed to have forged signatures for power of attorney, making her a very rich woman. This practice allowed Dr. Hazzard to claim innocence when her patients would die, leaving her their money, property, and valuables, explaining that things went "horribly, horribly wrong" during their treatment. But people were getting suspicious, and loved ones were getting angry. The problem was that the authorities couldn't really do anything, for the people whom had died under Hazzard's care had gone to see her of their own free will, so the killings continued.

In September of 1910 two wealthy British sisters, Claire and Dorothea Williamson, came across an ad for Dr. Linda Hazzard's treatment in a Seattle paper while vacationing at the Empress hotel in Victoria, Vancouver Island. By February of 1911 they had checked into Wilderness Heights in what was to be a short holiday, but by August of that year things had taken a deathly turn for the worst.

It seems Claire had managed to send a cryptic telegram home begging for help, but before help could arrive, she had died weighing less then fifty pounds. Dr. Hazzard claimed that Claire died of the ailments she had sought treatment for and that when she arrived she was already close to death's door. It was Dr. Hazzard's autopsy that noted cirrhosis of the liver as the cause of death. These famous autopsies were performed in the bathtub of her home, and, as always, when it came to her patients' deaths, she would find a probable cause outside of the reality of starvation.

Help however did come in time for her sister Dorothea, weighing close to sixty pounds. It seems that when questioned on her status, even though at this time the doctor had already taken legal guardianship over her and stated that Dora was insane, Dora and the doctor had different opinions on her well being. Dora would alternate between begging to leave and wanting to stay, claiming the fasting treatment was healing her. It seems Hazzard had told Dorothea that it was Claire's dying wish for her to spend her last days in Hazzard's care.

Once word got out to their uncle about Dorothea's physical and mental status, he immediately took legal action that began the downfall of the doctor's affairs. Realizing things were getting dangerous for her, Dr. Hazzard agreed to release Dorothea for a fee, which at first was $2,000 but she eventually lowered it. Released and back home, Dorothea and her family continued to take action against the practices of Dr. Linda Hazzard. The British Vice-Consul put pressure on the Washington state government to prosecute Hazzard for murder; however the government insisted that it didn't have the funds! So Dorothea Williamson, now thoroughly recovered, willingly paid for the prosecution from her own pocket.

By 1912 the authorities had become involved and made their arrest. During the trial Dr. Hazard did have her friends and supporters. Several of these were heavily into Spiritualism and Theosophy. One witness was John Ivar Haglund, Ivar's father, who testified that even though his wife, Daisey, had been Hazzard's first Washington victim, he believed in her practice and still allowed his son to continue with her treatment. Others testified against her, telling how many had seen her in the gowns and jewelry of her dead patients. There were even claims that she and her husband, Sam, had pulled

List of known victims of Dr. Linda Hazzard

• 1908
Daisey Maud Haglund
Ida Wilcox

• 1910
Maude Whitney
Earl Edward Erdman

• 1911 [cont'd]
Lewis Ellsworth Rader
Claire Williamson

• 1909
Blanche B. Tindall
Viola Heaton
Eugene Stanley Wakelin

• 1911
Frank Southard
C.A. Harrison
Ivan Flux

• 1913
Ida J. Anderson
Mary Bailey

the victims' gold fillings and crowns and sold them to a local dentist. Even after the body of Eugene Stanley Wakelin, a man from a wealthy family, was found badly decomposed on the property with a gunshot wound to the head, the police suspected suicide, but others believed it was murder so Hazzard could collect the family fortune. In the end, the jury returned with a verdict of manslaughter instead of murder. It is believed that the jury refused to believe that a woman could do such a horrendous thing.

She was given two-to-twenty years in prison, which was served in the Washington State Penitentiary at Walla Walla. She was released on parole on December 26, 1915, and the following year Governor Ernest Lister gave her a full pardon. She and her husband then moved to New Zealand to continue her work as a health specialist. During this time she continued to write books that brought in enough money for her return to the United States ten years later.

In 1920, the doctor returned to Olalla to rebuild her fame, opening the School of Health in which she continued to starve patients until the school burned down in 1935. In the case of "physician heal thyself," it was discovered that the doctor had died of self-starvation in 1938.

Many might suggest Dr. Linda Hazzard had exercised the power of black magic or mind control over her victims. One reporter cautioned people to avoid looking into the doctor's eyes as she might bewitch them. As to how many might have fallen under her spell and died, the count has never been confirmed. Some report more than forty. In fact, it is believed that there are dozens of victims that will never be accounted for. Many of these unfortunate souls are believed to be buried on her old property, which today is reported to be haunted.

Ivar said he didn't remember much of his mother and was one of the lucky ones to escape with his life. He started his career as a folk singer and later made his fortune in the restaurant business. He then purchased the Smith Tower and at one time flew a fifty-foot-long salmon kite from the top until the wind carried it away one day.

In 1983, filing as a prank, he was elected port commissioner only to die of a heart attack just over a year later on January 30, 1985.

Many working on Pier 54 and in Ivar's restaurant believe that his pleasant spirit is still around watching over a world he created. If you are quiet enough, you just might catch him whistling, humming, or even singing a tune to one of his favorite folk songs.

See also: Butterworth's in Pike Place Market

THE H A U N T E D FERRY
801 Alaskan Way (at Pier 50)

On the Seattle to Bainbridge Ferry, just around dusk, folks have seen a frail old woman with her cane wander onto the ferry. She will sit down to rest her weary feet and remain there, sitting perfectly still. The odd thing is that she seems to never make it to the Bainbridge docking. Folks say she's never seen again. In some accounts, curious

THE HAUNTED FERRY

onlookers have asked the woman if it's all right to take her photo, but when they do so, she vanishes before their eyes. She has been described to be of Native American descent, and some believe this may very well be Princess Angeline trying to visit the village of her people for one last time.

THE SEA KING

This ship was the largest vessel ever built when completed in 1877—273 feet long with a capacity of fifteen hundred tons. The Sea King was built from lumber harvested and selected in Georgia by expert shipbuilders. It had many voyages around the world, but one voyage may have doomed it for good.

It was just after the great San Francisco earthquake of 1906, in which the Sea King had been docked and getting ready for a voyage north to Seattle. A ship of this size would take on landfill to fill the ship's ballast in order to help balance the ship during its voyage. After unloading lumber from Seattle, the ship restocked to head back to Seattle. At this time a lot of the material used to weigh the ship down was rubble from San Francisco's recent disaster.

The ship set sail with no troubles and made it back to Seattle to load up once more. It seems the crew had their own troubles, though, with complaints of disturbing noises, like groans from the bowels of the ship all night long to strange occurrences and uncomfortable feelings on the whole trip. This was odd to the crew who had been sailing on this ship for years. It wasn't until they started to unload the rubble in the ballast from San Francisco that they discovered remains of those who'd perished in the earthquake. Soon after that the ship was considered cursed and was retired.

PIER 70

2901 Alaskan Way

The younger generation may be familiar with this location due to a popular MTV show called *Real World*. Each season takes a group of young adults and places them in a house for a few months to live together. This pier is one of the places they lived, but there's more to this waterfront property than what we thought.

Built in 1902, this pier has been many things and now houses offices and retail tenants, including seafood restaurants. But very few know of its haunting. In 1933

PIER 70

dozens witnessed a Native American man walk along the water's edge, but to their shock, he vanished out of sight. But he's not the only one who's been sighted here. It is believed that if you happen to be in a very depressed state and wander out to this pier possibly thinking of suicide, a young sailor will appear and talk to you, convincing you that life is worth living. You will then walk away with a new view of life, but when you turn back to thank him, he's nowhere to be seen. Could this be the ghost of a young man who didn't take his own advice and in regret now lingers around the pier to help others in need?

MAYFLOWER
PARK HOTEL
405 Olive Way

Billed as one of Seattle's finest hotels, this luxurious hotel was built in 1927 as the Bergonian Hotel. Owned by Stephen Berg, who also owned the Claremont Hotel, the building underwent major renovations when it switched hands in 1974. Today you can still see one of the stained glass windows that sports the "B" from its past. This

MAYFLOWER PARK HOTEL

hotel also has a guest who has never checked out. In 1997 three guests complained about strange occurrences happening in room 1120. Could this unseen guest still be hanging out at this popular hotel?

THE CRYSTAL POOL

2033 Second Avenue

"Out with the old and in with the new." That statement really applies to the twenty-two-story Cristalla condominium apartments built in 2005. But with this new, there is a pinch of history. In the new design, they kept the terracotta facades on the north and east sides of the original building. Known as the Crystal Pool when it was built in 1914, it featured an indoor, 260,000-gallon, heated, saltwater swimming pool. By the late 1920s they had covered over the pool, converting the space

THE CRYSTAL POOL

into a boxing venue that ran until the late 1930s. During the 1920s and 1930s, it was used as a meeting hall for the KKK. It seems they brought in close to seventy thousand people to their rallies, but by the 1930s they had pretty much come to an end. In 1943 the building was converted to a Pentecostal church, Bethel Temple, but after the church's sixty-year run, the building was torn down in 2003.

When construction started, many workers had issues with tools turning on and off by themselves. These tools would also disappear and reappear in odd places. One worker heard sounds of frantic splashing in water. He followed the sound to find it coming from a wall. As he listened closer he found he was standing over what he described to be naked wet footprints going through the wall. There where six deaths by drowning when it was a pool, and two where under suspicion causes. Some reports say people have seen an all-white figure wandering through the main and basement floors. Could this be a member of the KKK in his white robes?

HOTEL COMMODORE

Second Avenue and Virginia Street

After sitting vacant since 2006, the Hotel Commodore came down in 2008, and many locals were happy to see it go. The land is now a parking lot, but the hotel was a flophouse before it closed. Guests who stayed there posted nothing but horrible reviews including dirty sheets, smelly rooms, and even blood stains on the walls. Locals had complained of shady people and drug deals going on outside the hotel.

Built in 1909 as the Hotel Nelson, it was popular during the gold rush. But like most hotels after the gold hype died down, it fell into despair.

HOTEL COMMODORE

Many guests spoke of ghosts haunting this building, including things moving, lights turning on and off, and dark figures coming down the stairs. With its history of bad guests, it very well may have held on to some negative energy that was left behind.

Before the building saw its last days, the first floor had been boarded up to prevent vagrants and trespassers from entering. Locals living in the area claimed to see strange lights and shadowy figures move across the rooms through the windows. In fact, these sightings led to calls for the authorities to investigate possible trespassing. But when the building was checked over, there was no sign of a living person inside.

CAROUSEL

Pier 57 on Alaska Way

Pier 57 was built in 1902. This pier has witnessed a lot of history, including the docking of the *Miike Maru* in 1896, which opened trades with Japan, the *S.S. Portland* with its two tons of gold that launched the 1897 Gold Rush. But with its history also comes its ghosts.

Stories say that a young boy haunts the carousel and arcade on this pier. The child has been known to appear riding the carousel and playing the game machines. At night the carousel has been known to turn on and off on by itself. A woman saw

CAROUSEL

the child wandering through the arcade late one night. She called to him to ask where his parents were only to see him vanish. He has been described as wearing a white T-shirt and blue jeans. Supposedly a child drowned after falling off the pier. Could this be him?

JENSONIA HOTEL
1214 Eighth Avenue

The Jensonia Hotel, built in the 1920s and torn down in 2008, was an extended-stay hotel. Guests could check in and pay weekly rates or arrange for even longer stays. Like the days of Seattle's pioneers, and very much like many European accommodations, the rooms were small and cozy with shared bathrooms. Some might call this the perfect setting to experience things that go bump in the night. The building was very old and creaky, and the elevators looked like something from a horror film. Most people preferred to take the stairs.

Located in a poor area, the hotel had a number of untimely deaths within its walls, including murder, suicide, and drug overdoses. But nothing compared to the horrific events that led to the hotel's final days. It all began in January of 2004 when the hotel had a fire. This was the first of three fires in the hotel, with the second and third occurring in the same week that March. But the fires were just the prequels; greater tragedies occurred later that month.

In 2004, Lawrence Owens committed a murder, and the surrounding circumstances created great controversy. Owens was a convicted rapist, a registered sex offender with a history of abusing

JENSONIA HOTEL

women, and he was working as a custodian at a YWCA shelter for women. Due to an oversight, Owens' employment agency failed to do a background check before placing him at the shelter.

In 1997 Owens had pled guilty to charges of assault after beating his girlfriend. He was also found guilty of possessing an illegal firearm, as he had held a gun to his girlfriend's head and threatened to kill her. In addition to these crimes, he was found guilty of assault with sexual motivation for beating and raping yet another victim. For all of these crimes, he was sentenced to nine years. After serving six, he was released in September 2003.

After his release, he took up residence at the Jensonia Hotel where he met Dori Cordova and her ten-year-old son. Owens became attached to Cordova, and they developed a relationship. On March 17, 2004, Owens shot Cordova to death at the Miller Community Center on Capitol Hill where they had been sent for shelter after the last fire at the Jensonia. Owens apparently had found somewhere else for them (Cordova and Owens) to live, but she was leaving the community center with her son to live in another shelter. Owens shot Cordova, and moments later, the police shot and killed Lawrence Owens.

Many tenants who lived at the Jensonia Hotel spoke of an "evil" that lived within its walls. Some claimed to see shadowy creatures or hear odd noises such as growling in their rooms. Perhaps these elements created a chain of events responsible for bringing the hotel to its end?

PARAMOUNT THEATRE
901 Pine Street

Built for film and vaudeville in 1927, this historic landmark seats 2,807 guests and has hosted some of Hollywood's biggest names and Broadway's hottest shows. It also features a 1927 Wurlitzer Theatre Pipe Organ. This grand theater is a sight to see in itself, but most venues like this tend to have ghosts for you to see as well.

It seems they have a resident ghost that the employees have named "Erie." Going to the theater was Erie and his wife's favorite past time. One day fate took him from his two biggest loves, the theater and his wife. After his death, his wife still continued her dates to the Paramount, pretending her husband was still at her side. This included buying the empty sit next to her for her departed husband. People would see her

PARAMOUNT THEATRE

talking to herself and walking through the lobby with her arm wrapped around air, as if it had been wrapped around her husband's arm. Many of her friends and family believed she had gone crazy with her obsession over Erie's passing, believing he had returned to watch over her. It wasn't too long after his death that she followed him to the grave, dying of natural causes.

Some think that Erie has stayed on to watch over the theater; some even say that after his wife's death, he didn't know how to join her, so he remains at the theater waiting for her to join him. Either way, Erie passes his time by keeping the employees busy with his pranks. He'll lock doors that shouldn't be locked. He'll shut lights off on employees. But his favorite is stalling and not letting the door open on the elevator. Funny thing is, all his playful pranks are mostly focused on the women. Maybe Erie isn't 100 percent dead.

FAIRMOUNT OLYMPIC HOTEL
411 University Street

The Fairmont Olympic Hotel is described as the center of society in Seattle. Many dances, proms, balls, receptions, and parties took place within the hotel's walls. The opening celebration of the hotel on December 6, 1924 was the crown jewel of the social season in Seattle. More than two thousand people attended the dinner and dance. The pleasures enjoyed by the societies of New York, Atlanta, and Philadelphia could now be had in the Pacific Northwest.

While the Fairmont Olympic may hold a special place at the center of society, the hotel's physical location is in the center of Seattle's downtown on the former site of the first campus of the University of Washington. However, this is also where the Pioneer Cemetery once settled. Before the university took claim to the land in 1861, it was here that the first settlers of Seattle had taken their final rest before being moved to other cemeteries.

Through the years, the Fairmont Olympic Hotel has experienced a number of renovations, most recently in 2005. With more than two hundred suites and twice as many hotel rooms, the beauty and charm of this gem continues to draw visitors from around the world. Famous guests include Herbert Hoover, John F. Kennedy, Elvis Presley, Joan Crawford, and Jimmy Hoffa. Special honors of the hotel included its status as the only AAA Five Diamond hotel in Washington and its listing on the National Register of Historic Places.

It seems that a woman in a white, flowing dress of the 1920s walks the halls of this grand hotel. She has also been spotted sitting in the lobby. When guests and employees

FAIRMOUNT OLYMPIC HOTEL

notice her, she just fades into thin air. Some also talk about hearing 1920s music coming from nowhere. Perhaps events from the hotel's grand opening are replaying themselves? Others claim that Shuckers Restaurant inside the hotel may have a few spirits of its own. Here glasses and chairs move at their own free will. With so much history, could there be ghosts here? Maybe former guests have returned, or it could have something to do with the cemetery that is now part of the building foundation?

See also: University of Washington in University District

Haunting Fact

Animals tend to react to unseen forces by staring off or aggressively barking or meowing at what appears to be nothing. It is believed that animals can sense these spirits or "energies" around us. But through further research we now believe that it may not be a psychic impression but more of really seeing or hearing these encounters. We know that animals do see differently and also hear better than humans, so maybe they can see and hear these forces better than we can.

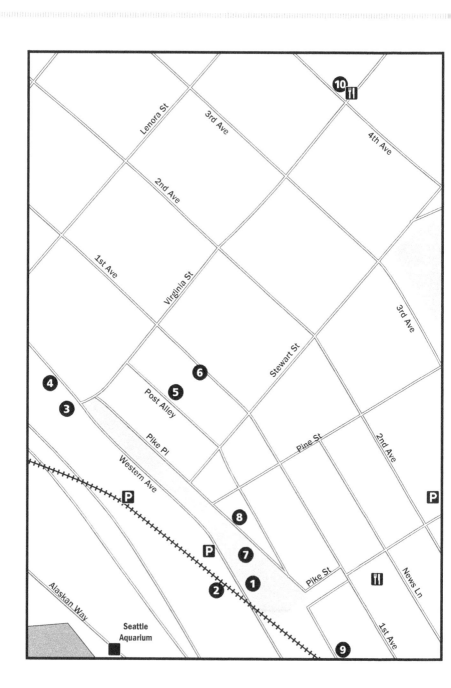

4. PIKE PLACE MARKET

Founded in 1907 as a farmers market, Pike Place Market is one of Seattle's most famous must-see locations. With a huge collection of interesting shops, shoppers can browse for antiques, fresh foods, and entertainment. The Pike Place Market is the oldest continuously operating and most historically authentic public market in the country. There was a time when the Market was threatened with demolition, but the people of Seattle voted in 1971 to establish a seven-acre Pike Place Market Historical District and a Market Historical Commission to preserve its physical and social character as "the soul of Seattle."

Some of the most famous attractions include: the first Starbuck's location, complete with the original and controversial sign with the bare-breasted siren; The Pike Place Fish Market where mongers throw the world-famous flying fish; and the statue of Rachel the Pig.

MAP MARKERS

1. A Point
2. Heritage House
3. Victor Steinbrueck Park
4. Cutters Bayhouse Restaurant
5. Kell's Pub
6. Butterworth's
7. Bead Zone
8. Mr. D's
9. Market Theatre
10. Claremont Hotel

PRINCESS ANGELINE

This blue-eyed Native American princess was born in 1820 to Chief Seattle, his oldest daughter. She lived out her life in a ten-by-ten-foot shack on the waterfront on Western Avenue just across the street from the Pike Place Market. There she would do carvings and weave baskets for the Ye Old Curiosity Shop on the pier. She was named Princess due to her father's status, and Angeline was given to her by Catherine Broshears Maynard, second wife of Seattle pioneer Doc Maynard. Her birth name was Kikisoblu Seattle or Sealth. She married Dokub Cud, who died before the arrival of Euro-American settlers. This woman had gained fame all over the world, for if you ventured to Seattle, you'd be sure to see her frail figure on the streets of Seattle selling her goods. One of the most popular tourist souvenirs was that of a Native American doll resembling Princess Angeline. She became the symbol that linked the past with the present. Although she died May 31, 1896 at the age of seventy-six, some say she has refused to leave even after her physical death. Yet, as with the forced removal of her people to reservations, she was spiritually bound to her homeland and there she would stay. Treaty or no treaty!

PRINCESS ANGELINE ON STREET CORNER

A POINT

Western Avenue (behind the market)

This sculpture was designed by artist Michael Oren in 1992. Its purpose is to mark a location that the Native Americans believed to be a very sacred place, and indeed it was. The point on this sculpture is believed to be where two worlds, the spirit world and the physical world, collide. There are also a few white stones beneath the sculpture; these are crystals that are supposed to increase one's sensitivity by rubbing them. Most people feel a tingling sensation or even a pressure in the palm of the hand when they bring their hands to the tip of the point. Could this be a doorway to the heavens or spiritual plane? Some may even believe this could be the work of connecting ley lines, which are lines of energy that run all over the Earth's crust. When these lines cross each other, they can build up concentrated energy. Whatever is happening here has had the power to change even the skeptic's mind.

HERITAGE HOUSE

1533 Western Avenue

This retirement home across from the Pike Place Market was built in 1990. Late at night, residents awake to find an elderly woman with piercing blue eyes and a fierce

HERITAGE HOUSE

glare standing at the foot of their beds. The residents would scream only to find her vanishing before their eyes. Night nurses would occasionally see elderly folks wander around in the middle of the night when they had trouble sleeping. So it was their job to get them back into their rooms and into bed. But on some occasions, when they'd find an elderly woman wandering the halls and the nurses would go to fetch her, to their surprise, she was nowhere to be found. Witnesses have said she appears to be an old Native American woman.

Through research, it was found that on the very spot where the Heritage House was built, Princess Angeline had settled in a ten-by-ten-foot hut on a pile of oyster shells to live out her remaining years, and that's where she died. Here is where she did her daily work, doing laundry for locals and making baskets for the tourists.

VICTOR STEINBRUECK PARK
2001 Western Avenue

This 0.8 acre park designed by Richard Haag, was built in 1978 on top of a parking garage once known as Market Park until it received its new name in 1985. It was named after a Seattle architect, Victor Steinbrueck, who was instrumental in the

VICTOR STEINBRUECK PARK

preservation of Pike Place Market and Pioneer Square. Here you will also see the twin totems that were carved by Quinault sculptors Marvin Oliver and James Bender. This piece of land is a favorite spot due to the amazing view looking out over Elliot Bay and the Olympic Mountains in the distance. Before the creation of the park, however, it was the former site of the Washington National Guard Armory, which was built in 1909, and it was damaged by fire in 1962. It attracts young people in business suits, homeless people in rags, and everyone in between.

On one occasion, a young couple came here to enjoy the sunset. While sitting on the bench, holding hands and cuddling, a homeless woman walked up to the couple and asked for some spare change. The gentleman wanted her to leave quickly, so he reached into his pocket and gave her all the change he had. When the coins where dropped into the woman's hands, surprisingly all that change went right through her hands and landed at the couple's feet. Right then the homeless woman disappeared into thin air. Apparently this woman has been seen wandering through the park—and then she vanishes. There have been many cases of the homeless dying in this park due to illness or drugs throughout the years.

Are the spirits of the unfortunate souls still hanging out among the living here at Victor Steinbrueck Park? If stopped by a homeless person asking for change, be conscious of who's got their hand out.

CUTTERS BAYHOUSE RESTAURANT

2001 Western Avenue

Known for its fine seafood dinning, Cutters also offers its guests a scenic view of the bay. But what most people don't know is that it also can offer a good ghost story as well. Wait staff and cooks have seen their fair share of oddities here, from a shadowy figure to dishes moving on their own. One story says that when they were hosting a wedding, a Native American woman appeared in front of the guests asking them to be quiet, but when addressed, she vanished, scaring everyone into a panic. It is believed that this Native American was the famous Princess Angeline.

On an AGHOST investigation at Cutters Bayhouse, a strange light formation was captured in the banquet room where the frantic occurrence took place. Plus the

CUTTERS BAYHOUSE

phenomena of EVPs of a female voice were recorded. In one recording you hear a woman saying "Thank you" in response to investigators taking a picture. Another recording captured an elderly woman laughing in the woman's restroom.

See also: Princess Angeline in this section

KELL'S PUB
1916 Post Alley

The pub is located on the ground floor of the Butterworth Building. With its address in Post Alley, Kell's faces the direction of Pike Place Market, but if you look above the entrance, you can see the fading letters of the Butterworth Building. The ground floor of the Butterworth Building operated as the hayloft, garage, and stables for the horse-drawn hearses that were also used as early ambulances to retrieve ascendant victims. This rear funeral entrance would have seen a lot of corpses coming and going through its doors as it was common practice to transport the dead in more isolated areas as to not upset the public. Here the corpses were brought in for preparation, loaded in the elevator to the third floor for embalming, and from here they were dispatched to their final resting places.

The Pub opened in October 1983 just in time for the Halloween festivities. Folks say that any time at Kell's feels like a celebration. Warm and cozy, both pub and restaurant have the feeling of another place and time. Kell's is always crowded, with patrons crammed elbow to elbow. Just be sure the elbow you rub up against is of this world and not the next.

For those who want a breath of fresh air or who daren't chance meeting up with a ghost, there is also an outdoor seating area where you can almost feel the vibes from the nearby Pike Place Market. If you look up you will see the faded letters of Butterworth & Sons painted along the top of the building.

The ghosts that haunt Kell's include a little girl with long hair. She has been seen wandering the bar area and playing games with the staff. One bartender saw a glass slide across the bar on its own. Another bartender had the bar closed and looking nice, but when he stepped over to the restaurant side to let co-workers know he was leaving, he returned to find all the chairs pulled out from the tables when there was no one around to do such a thing. Workers also say that when the bar is quiet, you sometimes hear the laughter of a child.

One story is that when a woman came in for a job interview, she brought her young daughter with her. During the interview she told her daughter to go play while she talked with the manager. The woman and the manager sat at a corner table while the child played throughout the bar. Within minutes the little girl came back to her mother to present a knotted-up rag that appeared to resemble a doll. The woman was confused as to where her daughter got such a thing or even how she might have learned to make the doll. The mother asked her child where she got the rag. Her daughter pointed to a secluded area and told her that a little girl with long, red hair showed her how to do it and gave her the doll. Shocked, the mother and manager told the child that there was no other little girl at the bar. Her daughter persisted that there was indeed a new little friend for her in the back. Both the mother and the manager proceeded to the back, but found no sign of any other child. They returned to the table after instructing the woman's daughter to go play once again. After some time passed the mother looked around to see what her daughter was doing. When she couldn't see her, she then called for her. There was no reply. Both the mother and manager began searching the bar and found her sitting on the floor talking to an invisible presence while playing with the rag doll. The frightened mother grabbed her child by the arm and left and was never heard from again.

As to who this little girl could be, she may very well trace back to the building's past and a time when children often died very young. Is she someone who died in Seattle and her funeral was held here at Butterworth & Sons?

The other ghost is a man they call Charlie. His spirit is mostly seen in the Guinness mirror, closest to the back bar. Many have seen an older man in a derby hat. He will be there for a few seconds and then vanish. These reports came in from many of the guests and visiting band members. It seems they most often see him while performing to an audience of the living and even the dead.

For the owners and employees, stories of the strange encounters are heard quite often and are even experienced firsthand for themselves. From ghostly voices yelling at the living, to a redheaded woman roaming the floors in search of something, to shadows pacing back and forth along the back walls—you're never alone in this building as the unearthly dwellers keep an eye on all who venture in.

With the building rich in funereal history, there very well could be more ghosts attached to this building. One thing for certain is that many unsuspecting guests do not like to hang out at the back bar, where most activity seems to occur.

BUTTERWORTH'S

1921 First Avenue

Edgar Ray Butterworth had moved to the Washington area from Massachusetts after loosing his wife in childbirth, taking up residence in the town of Centerville (today know as Centralia). Here he was the mayor; he ran an inn, a flower mill, and even a small furniture store that occasionally sold coffins due to the great demand. It seems Mr. Butterworth had his hands in many things. It wasn't until 1889 that he first became an official mortician by heading up Cross Undertaking in Seattle, and three years later bought out the business in 1892. A well-respected man, he was known to forgive unpaid funeral debts at the end of each year. He was also the first to offer his funeral services to the local Asian communities when no one else would. From 1892 to 1903 there were a few Butterworth locations: two were on Front Street (First Avenue) before the rebuilding of Seattle, and two were on Pike Street, one on Third, and the other on Fourth.

By 1903, almost four years before Pike Place Market started, Butterworth moved his funeral business to the First Avenue property. Butterworth had this building designed to be home to his business and offices (*No*, he did not live here). This was

BUTTERWORTH BUILDING

also the first building to be built exclusively for funeral services. For twenty years, the Butterworth business thrived on First Avenue. In March of 1923, the family business moved to Capitol Hill.

The brick building is long and narrow, with approximate dimensions of thirty feet wide by one hundred feet deep. The structure appears larger from the back view, which faces the Pike Place Market. Kell's Irish Pub is located on the first floor, and on the upper levels one can see the faded letters that advertised the business. From the back, the building has five floors including the ground floor. From the First Avenue view, there are three floors. The entrance from First Avenue remains fairly intact, complete with the tiled floors leading visitors to their destinations as marked: office, chapel, and private (the entrance to the upstairs offices).

Dr. Linda Hazzard of Starvation Heights fame was believed to have disposed of her victims here by having them cremated immediately so no one could see the horrendous abuse she had put them through. In fact, the Butterworths were implicated in the notorious murder case because they had cremated Clair Williamson, and then produced a less emaciated body for identification. However, charges were never brought against the Butterworth family.

Much of the building's beauty is as it was when the Butterworth business operated here: woodwork, brass, and the tiling. The building is listed in the National Historic Register. Beyond the physical riches of the art and design of the building, the family left behind some of their former customers. Many visitors to this property swear that the place is Seattle's most haunted.

Through the many years, this building has stood here. Quite a few businesses have tried to operate from what should be a great location, only to fail within two years or less. Many employees have quit due to odd activity. One cook left right in the middle of a dinner service after pots and pans flew off a shelf at him. Bartenders have seen wine and champagne bottles explode for no reason. Wine glasses have been known to fly across the room crashing on the opposite wall, and door knobs rattle and shake as if to get someone's attention.

The most commonly reported apparition is that of a woman, who will wander through the restaurant staring at guests and employees. Although she makes folks feel very uncomfortable, when approached, she just vanishes.

Another story of an apparition includes an older couple dinning in a booth when this site was known as Avenue One. At that time, the restaurant had a long, red velvet curtain in front of the hallway entrance. As the gentleman was facing the curtain, he saw a hand pull the curtain back, revealing a woman behind it. To his shock, he discovered she had no legs as she floated above the ground. She then glanced at him and calmly shut the curtain.

There is also the story of a male heard singing from time to time. This very well could be Fred Ray "Buzz" Butterworth, who had been known to sing for guests during funeral services.

ODD LIGHT FORMATION

Women visitors have felt the presence of a man in the ladies' restroom. A few times, he was spotted for just an instant when a female opened the door and walked in. Startled, perhaps thinking they had walked into the men's restroom, they dashed out to double-check only to find that it was indeed the ladies. Reentering the ladies room, they found him gone. Some women have had the frightening experience of sitting on the toilet when he walks in, only to find him gone once they open the stall door. It was discovered that when renovations were done on the building, the restrooms were switched to accommodate the women needing a larger restroom.

Throughout the years, there have been tons of ghost stories that have stemmed from this location. In 2009, AGHOST experienced some odd activity during an investigation. A psychic felt the presence of the woman and told the team to focus its attention on the balcony. One member did so, as the rest concentrated on the lower floor. During this time, the member on the balcony felt something yank his camera from his hand, and just moments later another member captured a photo of the balcony revealing a bright light formation above the member who was still fussing over his camera.

Other strange things experienced that night included feelings of cold spots and recordings of strange sounds and voices responding to questions. Could these be the spirits of the old funeral home who have chosen to stay behind and watch over the living?

See also: Ivar and the Doctor in Waterfront; Chapel Bar in Capitol Hill

BEAD ZONE

1501 Pike Place, Apt. 75 (inside the market)

When this bead shop moved into the market, they weren't expecting to have ghosts hanging out in their store. For years stories have circulated about sightings of a young boy or even a Native American woman haunting this shop. Stories seem to be that the child loved to play with the beads: he throws them at customers; strings of beads will fly off the walls; and things disappear when needed most. The spirit of the young prankster had been so active that they decided to call him Jacob. When the new owners moved in and took over the bead shop, they made some small renovations. There had been a door painted shut for many years, and the new owner was curious about what might be on the other side. Once the door was forced open, they reported an icy breeze passing by as if something or someone ran past them. To their surprise, a small room filled with junk was behind the door, but there was also a basket of missing beads and a few small toys. Could this have been Jacob's hiding spot? The shop has moved from this location to another spot in the market.

BEAD ZONE

MR. D'S

1518 Pike Place Market

In the tradition of the Greek-style kabob, Mr. D offers his customers a new look to their meat. In his shop, he carves pounds of meat into busts of famous people. Captured in meat are the likes of Jay Leno, Bill Clinton, and many other familiar faces. Unfortunately, not all his works of art survive the overnight storage. It seems that

MR. D'S

when Mr. D leaves his projects in the downstairs walk-in refrigerator, he often returns in the morning to find his meat faces almost destroyed. Ears and noses are cut off, or the bust is disfigured as if someone snuck in late at night to vandalize the sculptures.

Even if someone had overnight access to the refrigerator, who would do such a cruel thing to Mr. D's meat sculptures? Mr. D's belief is that he has two spirits living on his property. He thinks that these two ghosts fight with each other, and during their fighting, his meaty sculptures get in the way. Employees do not like to go down to the refrigerator alone in fear of running into these angry ghosts. Maybe the ghosts will want to continue their meat carving by cutting off the ears of an employee!

MARKET THEATER
1428 Post Alley

This small theater is hidden away down Post Alley. The one giveaway to its location is the world-famous Gum Wall—a wall on which millions of pieces of gum cover every brick. In fact, it has been voted number two as the world's most germ-infested location. In 1907 the theater was a stables that housed the horses of the vendors who sold at the market. In 1977 it was converted into a movie house that included a brass front door from a theater in New York and carpet from the original Radio City Music Hall lobby. When it didn't provide a profit, it was closed in 1989 and then reopened in 1991 for Unexpected Productions Improv.

Cast members have seen odd things happen. At times the piano will strike a few keys; a woman in 1920s attire was seen in the lobby as well as a man in a bowler hat. During one investigation by AGHOST, the psychic picked up on the woman and claimed the woman died from being kicked in the head by a very large animal. It is very possible she may have been kicked by one of the horses when it was a stable. Another investigation recorded sounds of walking on the stage when no one was around.

The theater also has a section in the audience seats that they refer to as "the crying corner." This section

MARKET THEATER

is set aside for guests who may have a crying baby or are under the weather. They say that if someone sits in those seats, they will cry for no apparent reason.

CLAREMONT HOTEL
2000 Fourth Avenue

First known as the Claremont Apartment Hotel built in 1925, during an era when hotels took a new direction by offering kitchens and private baths. So some hotels could act as an apartment building as well. The 283-room, ten-story building was anticipated to cost $700,000 and was the second to be built in downtown in this fashion in the mid-1920s.

The Claremont served as a transfer station for members of the Women's Army Corps during the late 1940s. It is believed that some time in the 1960s, a woman had fallen to her death on the ninth floor. In 1973 the building had a fire after which major repairs had to be done. It became a co-op in the 1980s and was converted into a conventional tour-and-travel hotel in 1987. In 2004 the building experienced major renovations, which turned it into a modern, lavish hotel now known as the Hotel Andra.

Employees and guests complain about the loud partying on the ninth floor, which stops abruptly whenever anyone investigates and then continues when they leave. Witnesses say that it sounds like a party from the Roaring Twenties, judging from glasses crashing and the jazz music. Witnesses have seen a paperweight float into the air and then suddenly drop, breaking the glass-top desk.

HOTEL ANDRA

On one occasion, guests saw a woman appear in their room on the eighth floor, only to see her vanish in front of their eyes. Stories say that a woman had committed suicide on this floor, and many have seen her spirit roaming the area. More guests have seen a shadow of a man standing in their room. One employee asked in fear, "How do you turn off a ghost?"

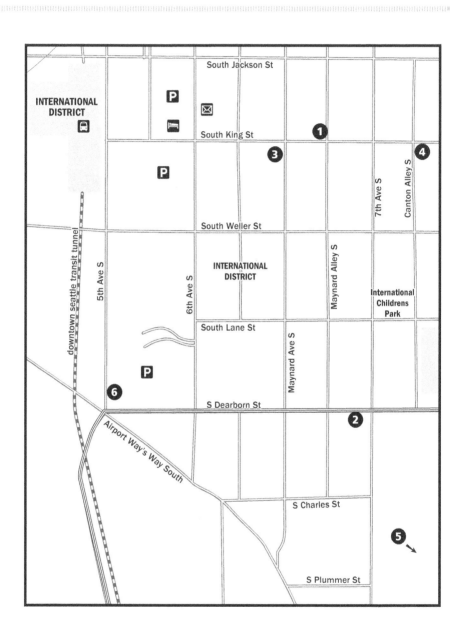

INTERNATIONAL
DISTRICT

South Jackson St

South King St

South Weller St

INTERNATIONAL
DISTRICT

South Lane St

S Dearborn St

Airport Way's Way South

S Charles St

S Plummer St

downtown seattle transit tunnel

5th Ave S

6th Ave S

Maynard Ave S

Maynard Alley S

7th Ave S

Canton Alley S

International
Childrens
Park

5. INTERNATIONAL DISTRICT

As one of the city's oldest neighborhoods, the International District was founded as Chinatown in the 1880s. Located on the eastern fringe of Pioneer Square, this area was mostly populated with Chinese immigrants who were recruited to help lay the area's first railroads, dig its coal mines, and can its salmon harvests. (continued next page)

MAP MARKERS

1. Wah Mee Club
2. Hong Kong Bistro
3. Mary Pang Warehouse
4. The Wing Luke Museum
5. Amazon.com Building
6. I-90

CHINATOWN GATE

Today Chinatown lies at the heart of the International District. Sometimes referred to as I.D., the International District is rich with history and culture. For many years, this neighborhood has served as the cultural hub for Asian Americans in Seattle. With its ethnic restaurants, unique specialty shops, and diverse heritage sites, these many attractions represent the diverse cultures coexisting in this neighborhood. One of the major attractions of this area is the Historic Chinatown Gate.

Also of note, this neighborhood houses the location of the former Wah Mee Club, site of the Wah Mee Massacre, where thirteen people were killed in 1983.

THE HUNGRY GHOST FESTIVAL

The Chinese take this popular event very seriously. On the fifteenth day of the seventh month of the lunar calendar, the Chinese community in Malaysia celebrates the release of spirits from purgatory. People believe that the gates of hell are opened to free the hungry ghosts of their ancestors and that these spirits wander the earth in search of food until the thirtieth day of the month. Under their blend of Buddhist, Confucian, and Taoist religions, the Chinese believe that their ancestors can influence their joss (luck) in this life. If you explore the Chinese quarter of Penang, there are small offerings left to the spirits wherever you look. Bowls of noodles, sweetmeats, cakes, and other treats are left in public places, while paper effigies of daily items are burned for spirits to use in the afterlife. In addition to edible goodies, street corners positively buzz with Chinese opera stage shows and puppet shows.

On what is one of Seattle's ugliest pages in history, we find the shameful act of more than two thousand angry men. Secretly coming together in the early morning hours of February 7, 1886, this mob of citizens systematically went from dwelling to dwelling attempting to force all Chinese immigrants to leave Seattle.

Chinese laborers had been part of the landscape for some time. The first appearance of the Chinese in the Pacific Northwest belonged to those who arrived as part of Captain John Mears' crew when he landed in Nootka Sound on Vancouver Island in 1789.

Two of Mears' projects were the Northern Pacific Railroad and the Oregon Improvement Company; each of these developments was instrumental in bringing

HUNGRY GHOSTS FESTIVAL

the Chinese north from California. More development on America's western frontier increased the demand for a cheap labor force. With so many laborers seeking work, many began migrating north to Seattle as the city's economy grew throughout the next century.

While many were happy to reap the labors of the workers, many citizens were unhappy with the influx of their Chinese neighbors. The movement of Chinese into the area apparently caused such resentment in white citizens that property values fell, and the city's business district grew in an unnatural direction. The Chinese were barely tolerated and never treaded as equals. In 1882, a separate school was established for Chinese children at the Methodist Episcopal Church at Fourth and Columbia; about forty children attended.

Tensions continued to build between the Chinese community and some of their more vocal adversaries, and violence began in the late summer of 1885. The Knights of Labor, one of the largest labor organizations of the nineteenth century, was responsible for many of the disturbances. They complained that the cheap labor supplied by the immigrant workforce was a threat to the skilled labor of their members and threatened to do something about the situation.

In the dark hours between Saturday evening and Sunday morning, February 7, 1886, a mob invaded the Chinese quarter and quietly entered the homes of Chinese residents. Once inside, the occupants were dragged from their beds, told to dress and pack their personal belongings. The mob had carts ready to carry these belongings to a steamer waiting to take all of their detainees to California. However, the captain of the vessel insisted that he would only take those who could pay the fare. Of the more than four hundred shocked and frightened men on the dock, fewer than eighty had enough for their passage.

By this time, the sheriff had arrived and was so outnumbered by the mob that he was forced to deputize other willing citizens to assist with crowd control. The mob was ordered to disperse, and after some struggle, they willingly did so. However, they reassembled the next day and physical confrontations resulted in the serious injury of four persons and a single death.

The situation had no satisfactory solution. A few arrests of suspected leaders were made and meetings were forbidden in the city limits without the expressed permission of the brigadier general. Troops patrolled Seattle for weeks and stood ever at the ready to prevent another attack.

WAH MEE CLUB
Maynard Alley South (just south of South King Street)

On Feb. 18, 1983, three young male immigrants from Hong Kong entered the Wah Wee Club, operated illegally as an exclusive gambling club in a basement in a predominantly Chinese neighborhood. Fourteen victims, including club regulars, wealthy restaurant owners, and employees of the establishment were hog-tied, robbed, and shot in cold blood around the neck and head. Thirteen died, but a dealer at the club survived and later testified against the men. The men were identified as Kwan Fai "Willie" Mak, Wai-Chiu "Tony" Ng, and Benjamin Ng. Apparently Mak and his accomplices were able to enter the building because they had become known and trusted by the people at the club. Once inside, their intent was to leave no witnesses. This event was listed as Seattle's worst mass murder in the city's history.

Benjamin Ng and Willie Mak were charged with thirteen counts of aggravated first-degree murder. Tony Ng was acquitted of murder, but convicted of thirteen counts of first-degree robbery and a single count of assault with a deadly weapon.

WAH MEE GAMBLING CLUB

Each robbery charge brought a minimum sentence of five years to be served consecutively.

Today, the club has been locked up and undisturbed since that tragic night. Many feel that those killed that night still linger, reliving that horrible event. You will find few people who live in the area willing to go near the building. Strange noises have been heard, shadowy figures have been seen, along with faces appearing in the windows. Some folks have said they can hear the sounds of gunfire. It is believed the site may be a kind of resting place for those murdered there. Whatever may be occurring, there may linger a mystery for some time until someone is willing to reopen the doors to the underground tomb.

MARY PANG WAREHOUSE

815 Seventh Avenue S

This location was set on fire on January 5, 1995 by Mary's adopted son, Martin, in an attempt to collect on the insurance. In one of Seattle's largest fires, in which ten firefighters fought, four were killed due to the floor collapsing under their feet. It took two days to recover their bodies. Martin was given a thirty-five-year prison sentence for manslaughter. Since then folks have claimed to hear the screams of the firefighters falling. Others have seen shadowy figures of men wandering around the area, which is now a parking lot. Is it possible that tragic event was somehow recorded to remind us of how short life can be? Today there is a monument in Occidental Park in Pioneer Square that honors the men lost on that tragic day.

MARY PANG WAREHOUSE

H O N G K O N G Bistro
511 Maynard Avenue S

This place was abandoned for almost eight years. Rumor has it that someone died in this location, so no one wanted to rent this spot in fear of bad juju. Now people have reported hearing strange noises. Others have claimed to have felt the presence from the spirit realm. Could the spirit of the one who passed away here still be hanging about?

HONG KONG BISTRO

THE W I N G LUKE MUSEUM
719 South King Street

Opening in 1967 and named after the first Asian American to be elected to the Seattle City Council (in 1962, only to serve three years due to his death in a tragic plane crash), this is the only museum related to Asian Pacific American history, culture, and arts. Friends and supporters donated funds to start the museum Wing Luke envisioned. It was originally located

WING LUKE MUSEUM

in a small storefront on Eighth Avenue. In 2008 the museum moved to a much larger site on King Street.

When they displayed a number of artifacts from different faiths together in the same display case, the display case shattered. Many believe this was the work of some very upset "energies."

AMAZON.COM BUILDING
1200 Twelfth Avenue S

Towering over Seattle as if to keep a watchful eye on the city stands a red brick Art Deco building that was built in 1932 as a Marine Hospital. Closed in 1987, it was later purchased by Amazon and renovated. Now the building serves as the dot.com corporate center for the company.

What do you think happens when you convert an old hospital into offices? The spirits here might fill you in. One popular story is of a nurse who is not seen but smelled. Very often employees on the first floor will come across a sweet smell of

AMAZON.COM BUILDING

perfume lingering in the halls. Not one person claims it to be their brand. Lights have been known to flicker or shut off for no reason. Late at night, doors can be heard slamming when no one is around. Throughout the rest of the floors, employees have claimed to be followed by the sound of what they describe as a squeaky gurney. Every time they hear it and turn around, the sound stops. Then when turning back and starting to walk once more, the sound starts back up and follows them. Could this possibly be a doctor, bored and looking for more patients? Whatever is going on here, employees will agree—this is one place you never feel completely alone.

I-90

West Bound

Just outside the International District is where I-90 and I-5 meet. If you take I-90 to Mercer Island you will have to cross the Floating Bridge—that is where our story takes place. It seems that on rainy nights, people driving across from Mercer Island to Seattle will happen to see a young woman walking alongside the bridge. Concerned folks have been known to pull over after passing in order to offer a ride or help. But once they look back, the young woman is gone.

In 1979 a young woman was reported missing. This happened at a time when women were known targets for serial killers like Ted Bundy and Gary

I-90 FLOATING BRIDGE

Ridgway. Throughout the investigation no hard leads where found, as if she had just vanished. However, in 1981 there was a sharp turn in the case. When work was being done on the Floating Bridge to remove a bulge that had developed over the years, workers discovered a car that had been resting at the bottom of the lake for quite some time. Inside were the remains that would soon be identified as the missing woman from 1979. As the investigation continued it was found that the young woman had been driving in stormy conditions at high speed the night she disappeared, striking the bulge on the bridge. This is what may have caused her car to flip over the railing and into the lake, ending her life.

It is possible that the walking woman seen along the bridge may have been this young woman, maybe trying to get home to her loved ones or trying to let people know where she was. The supporting factor is that the mysterious woman has never been seen since the body was discovered. Home at last, she can now rest in peace.

Haunting Fact

Many folks believe that haunting activity happens only at night. This is not true; activity can happen 24/7. People tend to notice most paranormal events when they are in relaxation mode. After we are done with the day's chores, are home from work, the dishes are done, and the kids are fed and off to bed, our senses increase as we are winding down. We will hear more sounds than when we were working out to AC/DC. Being busy throughout the day distracts us from our environment, and small amounts of activity can easily be overlooked.

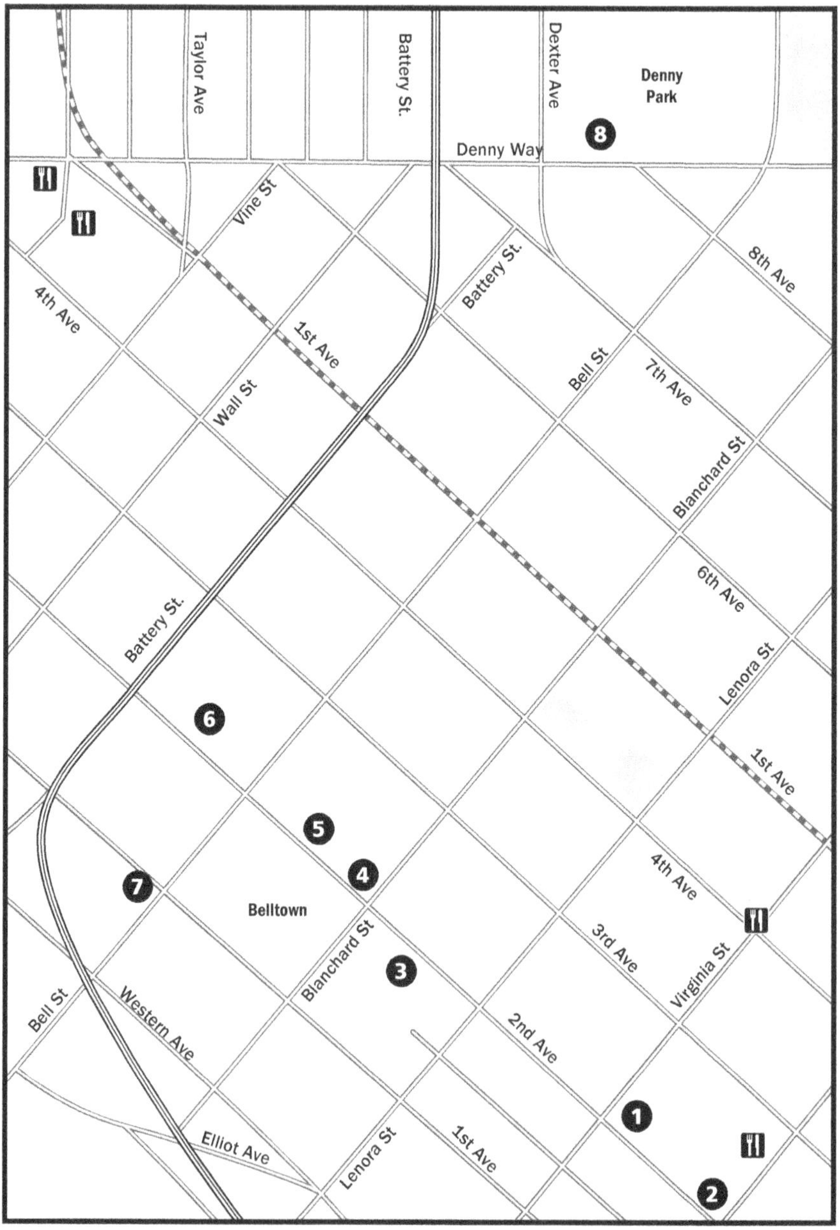

Taylor Ave

Battery St.

Dexter Ave

Denny Park

8

Denny Way

Vine St

Battery St.

8th Ave

4th Ave

1st Ave

Wall St

Bell St

7th Ave

Blanchard St.

Battery St.

6th Ave

6

Lenora St.

1st Ave

5

4

4th Ave

7

Belltown

Blanchard St.

3rd Ave

Virginia St.

3

Bell St

Western Ave

2nd Ave

1

Elliot Ave

Lenora St

1st Ave

2

6. BELLTOWN

Belltown is named after William Nathaniel Bell, a member of the Denny party, on whose land the neighborhood was built. This neighborhood fluctuates from low-rent to pricy to trendy. Formerly consisting of mostly industrial entities, the area became a playground for the wealthy and is now the home of the trendier bars and restaurants

Some of the more notable attractions in this neighborhood are Lava Lounge, Crocodile Café, and Olympic Structure Park.

MAP MARKERS

1. The Moore
2. The Josephinum
3. Rivoli Apartments
4. The Crocodile Café
5. Lava Lounge
6. The Rendezvous
7. Sophie Apartments
8. Denny Park

THE MOORE THEATRE
1932 Second Avenue

Built in 1902 by James A. Moore of Capitol Hill fame, this fancy building containing a hotel and theater was the hottest attraction in its day. Funny thing is, it was built so quickly that the day they opened their doors for the first performance, workers were still installing the seats. Now the building houses a moderately inexpensive hotel and

THE MOORE THEATER

Seattle's oldest and still popular theater that brings in big names and packs the seats. This place has also grown in popularity with its haunts. In fact, the team from SyFy's *Ghost Hunters* paid a visit here to film their Seattle investigations back in 2006.

Stories say that there is a seat in the audience that still carries the smell of cigars after many years, even though it has been reupholstered and even fully replaced during the building's many renovations. Today you can still smell the cigar smell every once in a while. Employees have heard the stories and have their personal experiences as well. One night after a show, some of the employees decided to wander into a back room to try to make contact with the ghosts by using a Ouija board. This went on for hours until the owner walked in on them. Upset, the owner fired them all right on the spot. Since then the owner admits to hearing a heavy breathing from an unseen force and hearing footsteps walking up and down the halls when no one is around. Reports abound of those feeling someone breathing down their necks or even being touched by unseen hands. There have also been reports of apparitions of a woman and a child being seen throughout the night wandering through the building's darkened empty hallways.

One couple checked into a room on the fourth floor. Late in the night the man woke up to odd noises in the room. As he looked around the darkened room, he saw to his horror a dark figure standing in the corner of the room. This caused him to freeze in fright as the figure drew closer to the bed. His eyes could not move from the shadowy figure nor could he yell to wake his girlfriend who was sleeping beside him. The figure crossed over to the other side of the bed and stood over his girlfriend. It then reached over and shook the bed. At that moment his girlfriend woke up and looked up at him and asked what was wrong. Still his eyes where locked on the shadowy image. She then turned to see what he was looking at, and as she did, it vanished before she could see what it was that terrified her boyfriend. They left that night.

THE JOSEPHINUM

1902 Second Avenue

This fourteen-floor luxury hotel was built in 1903 and opened in 1908. Towering over the Moore Hotel, it was later purchased by Mr. James A. Moore and renamed the New Washington Hotel. During the Great Depression, the building lost ownership

THE WASHINGTON HOTEL

and was left vacant for many years. In 1963, the Catholic Archdiocese of Seattle purchased the hotel and converted it into a retirement home. The building was opened up
to all low-income citizens in January 1990. The former hotel banquet room still bears
its original ornate terra-cotta ceiling and marble wall trim.

The Josephinum grounds have some interesting history. In 1853, the ground on
which it stands started out as one of Seattle's first cemeteries known as the Denny
Hotel Cemetery. If the cemetery ever had a formal name, it remains unknown as there
was none recorded. Burials were made informally at that time, and there wasn't even
a charge for a plot. By its end in 1860, the cemetery had about twenty bodies before
they where moved to the Seattle Cemetery (Denny Park).

In 1898, as construction started on the Denny Hotel, workers discovered two
Indian graves, recognizable as such by the burial goods with the bodies. In a Seattle PI
report on the findings, Arthur Denny had this to say: "Seattle's first burying ground
for the whites was located on the Denny Hotel grounds, about where Stewart Street

crosses Second Avenue. We buried there for several years, and also during the Indian War. Burials there were commenced as early as 1853 and continued as late as 1860." He also added that the graves had been removed when it was abandoned, but many of the graves had been neglected, and some very well could have been missed. He also stated that he had no knowledge of Indian graves at the site.

Denny Hotel was to be Seattle's grandest hotel as it towered over Seattle, offering guests the most beautiful scenic views in the West. But shortly after construction, funding was pulled in 1893, leaving an amazing empty shell hovering over the city for ten years. James A. Moore purchased it, had the interior completed, and changed its name to The Washington Hotel. One of this hotel's claims to fame is that President Theodore Roosevelt stayed in one of the grand rooms on his visit to Seattle. Moore was able to get two wonderful years out of his grand hotel being saved from the Great Seattle Fire before it became clear that the dirt under the grand Washington Hotel was more valuable than the building itself, so the hotel was torn down.

Today stories say that there is a young woman who appears and can be heard humming and singing in the stairway in the new building that now stands where the grand structure had once towered over Seattle. One account is that a man was visiting his grandmother who was living there at the time. As he stood in the lobby waiting for the elevator, he heard a slight humming draw closer and closer. Just then the elevator doors opened to reveal a young woman standing inside. Being gentlemanly, he tipped his hat to greet her, stepped inside, and turned to the panel to hit the button for the next floor. The doors closed, and the young woman began to hum behind him as the elevator proceeded up. His destination approached and the doors opened. At the same time, the woman stopped humming. He then turned to say good-bye to the young woman, and, to his surprise, there was no one there. He described the woman as having her hair in a bun, but messy, and she was in a dark dingy dress.

Many residents refuse to wander in the basement area alone for there is a very unwelcoming feeling down there. You can hear people talking, even when you know you are alone. Some have described smells of death like those in a funeral home. Many feel that what seems to lurk in the basement is left behind from the ground's time as a cemetery.

Could the young woman in the elevator be the spirit of a vagrant who died in the building while it was abandoned, or is she someone remaining from the pioneer cemetery?

RIVOLI APARTMENTS
2127 Second Avenue

The Rivoli Apartments were built in 1910 and designed by A. H. Albertson, who had a hand in many of Seattle's greatest buildings, including the Northern Life Building and St. Joseph Church. Some may be more familiar with it as it appeared in the Alan Rudolph film *Trouble in Mind*. The Rivoli was originally built to house many of the dockworkers. To keep the rent cheap for these low-income tenets, this apartment building offered small studios with Murphy beds. In the 1960s the building started its decline into despair, and by the 1980s it was barely livable for the living. But perhaps that's when the ghosts moved in.

The most famous ghost is a young Eskimo woman who arrived in Seattle in the early 1980s with the hope of starting a new life. Her relationship with a Cuban, Rudolfo, turned deadly when, after an argument in which he accused her of cheating, he stabbed her and hid her body inside the Murphy bed. He then paid the next

RIVOLI APARTMENTS

month's rent and left town. At this time, the management allowed padlocks to be used on the outside of the front doors for extra security, and so no one knew what had happened until eventually her decaying body was discovered when neighbors reported a foul smell coming from the apartment. In years since, residents of the building have reported a foul smell in the hallway, which seems to come from the apartment, and the woman's apparition has been reported roaming the building. Some have even claimed to have felt her or even seen her shadowy figure lurking about.

Another reported apparition is that of a woman named Christine, who died in a third-floor apartment in the mid-1980s. In her late thirties or early forties and in ill health, Christine reportedly had no friends or visitors and would purposely clog her plumbing and fuss with the wiring so that people would have to frequently visit her to fix what problems she may have caused herself. This would allow people to spend time with her in the apartment. Social workers attempted to convince her to move to a care facility, but she refused, and in the years since her death, it is reported that she still haunts the building, clogging the plumbing, flicking lights on and off, and flushing the toilets.

In the 1990s a television show did a ghost story on the Rivoli. They had a psychic walk through the building to see if she could make contact with any spirits. She didn't pick up on the murder that had taken place here or even the crazy woman who likes to flush toilets. However, she did pick up on two men she claimed had committed suicide together after being diagnosed with the AIDS virus. As sad as that might be, her premonitions did have a nice ending. She felt that the two men's spirits watch over everyone in the building, protecting them from any wrongdoings. This building has the lowest crime rate in the area. Could this be the work of those men watching over the people who call the Rivoli home?

THE CROCODILE CAFE
2200 Second Avenue

For many bands starting up in the Seattle area, the Crocodile Café is the rock 'n' roll venue to play.. In fact, bands like Pearl Jam and Nirvana played here in their early years. In 2008, The Crocodile closed it doors for good, but on its last night of business, Pearl Jam gave a farewell performance here. This was a very hush, hush event.

Shortly after the final day of the café, new owners bought it, remodeled it and opened its doors once again. But with the purchase, they obtained the ghosts as well. There have been stories of ghostly activity for years—a shadowy male figure lurking about in darkened corners, things being moved around, and lights going off and on by themselves.

CROCODILE CAFÉ

LAVA LOUNGE

LAVA
LOUNGE
2226 Second Avenue

The building itself dates back to 1890 and is believed to be the last remnant of Belltown's housing built before the Denny Hill Regrade. Once called Hawaii West, this old seafarers' bar was believed to be haunted by a young woman who would appear in the ladies' lounge. Reports of this young woman's appearance began surfacing in the 1980s when visitors to the lounge claimed to see a young woman huddled in the corner, sobbing. Many would approach the woman to ask if she needed assistance, but the young woman would ignore them and continue crying. Whenever someone asked an employee to check on the crying guest, she would disappear. Employees would go to check on her, but she was gone and would not be seen again in the same evening.

Those who saw the young woman described her as having long, dark hair and wearing a reddish-pinkish-colored dress. Following these sightings, a small group of amateur ghost hunters investigated the lounge in hopes of uncovering the mysterious young woman's identity. From their efforts, they produced photographs with images that they describe as reddish-pinkish orbs, matching the colors of the crying woman's dress.

The young crying woman's last sighting was in 1989. Little is known of this woman: who she was or why she was crying. We can only hope that her failure to reappear means that she has moved on.

THE RENDEZVOUS

2322 Second Avenue

Rendezvous, with its JewelBox Theater, first opened in 1924. It's the kind of club that some might call a dive while others call it a hidden gem. The place feels luxurious with its rich colors and designs, velvet wall hangings and chandeliers. Some might say it feels like an old Hollywood movie theater. Inside the space are many areas, including the main room with an upstairs loft, the Grotto in the basement and the JewelBox Theater.

In the 1940s, the space was converted into one of the film houses of Seattle's famed Film Row. From the 1920s to the 1960s, Second Avenue was called Film Row with a large number of screening houses and the Film Exchange Building taking up an entire block of Second Avenue, from Battery Street to Wall Street. B.F. Shearer operated it, until he closed its doors in 1972. After that it had changed hands and venues, even operating as a porno theater.

Today, The JewelBox Theater is the only screening room to continue showing films. Patrons can also enjoy a number of live performances. The JewelBox Theater has the feel of a vaudeville house, with its intimacy and red velvet curtains. Comedy, burlesque, and various musical acts frequent the stage, and audiences love it.

People's opinions of Rendezvous vary. Some remember a seedier version of the bar and miss it, while others feel its current state captures more of the glamour and elegance of its history. Ghosts certainly feel right at home here. Some people have seen a man in the old projection room, turning on the projectors and locking the doors, making it almost impossible to enter and turn off the films. Performers have seen his shadowy figure looking out the viewing window.

Some rumors say that one of the ghosts could be the well-known actor and comedian Jimmy Durante, "The Nose," who died in 1980. During Prohibition, movie moguls and celebrities like Durante played cards at the speakeasy in the basement. After reviewing his films, he would step out for a game of cards and a few drinks. However, no one has given a clear description of the ghosts seen here. If it is Durante, I don't think anyone could miss that nose.

Some have felt the presence of a woman throughout the building. Many have described a sweet-smelling perfume. An employee was working upstairs in the Red Velvet Lounge when a menu was ripped from his hands by unseen forces.

The most disturbing ghostly presence is the basement. Many have felt a very dark energy lurking in the darkened corners. Unexplained sounds of crashing and banging

THE RENDEZVOUS

have been heard. Others have described a feeling of panic coming over them, as if something were out to get them. It seems that the activity reported here has been so extreme that some employees won't talk about it or even venture ever again into the building's lower level.

Whoever haunts this old building, they have no intention of leaving any time soon. So if you choose to hang out at Rendezvous, just sit back and see what you might experience for yourself.

SOPHIE APARTMENTS
409 Denny Way

(MAHONEY TRUNK MURDER)

This neighborhood of Belltown thrived in the 1920s. The wealthy were buying up and constructing hotels, apartments, and businesses. Kate Mooers, a sixty-eight-year-old woman living in the area, owned an apartment building known as the New Baker House on First Avenue (that has since been destroyed by the construction of Highway 99). She later purchased another on Denny Way. Needing help running both properties, she hired Nora Mahoney. This was a life-changing decision, as it was shortly after that she met Mahoney's thirty-six-year-old son, James E. Mahoney, the man she would fall in love with.

From the beginning of their romance, the two were an unlikely pair. He was affable, young, and handsome, while she was much older, not very attractive (short and some said balding), and not thought to be very nice. In fact, Kate had a reputation for being quite the miser. A fairly recent divorcée, Kate was estimated to be worth hundreds of thousands of dollars, but she lived in a small apartment in the building she owned known as Sophie Apartments. A former brakeman for the railroad and now recently out of prison, James hadn't very much money. He was staying with his mother, Nora, who managed the New Baker property. Kate and James met in the building managed by Nora and had a whirlwind courtship. In less than two months, they were married in a small civil ceremony.

Two months after their wedding, Kate announced that she was taking her new husband on a belated honeymoon. They would leave by train for St. Paul, Minnesota, on April 16, 1921 and be gone for a month. Kate made the travel arrangements, withdrew almost two thousand dollars from her bank account and purchased nearly five hundred dollars' worth of travelers' checks.

While Kate made travel plans, James made other arrangements. He purchased morphine from the local druggist, a steamer trunk large enough for a body, some strong rope, and quicklime. He also sought out rental properties and boats along the lake, inquiring about the deepest part of the lake, claiming that he planned to do some fishing with a buddy.

Kate and James left their apartment on the evening of April 16t, but Kate was never seen again. James returned to Seattle less than two weeks later, claiming that Kate planned to continue her travels eastward to Boston, New York, and Havana, Cuba. He also claimed that Kate had sent him back to Seattle with power of attorney in hand to oversee her business affairs.

Family and friends did not know what to think of James' return without Kate nor his sudden spending habits. Considering Kate's tight control on her purse strings, it seemed rather odd that James would suddenly wear new suits, drive Kate's car, and paint the town red—all without his wife. When Kate's nieces, Kate Stewart and Carrie Hewitt, received strange letters from their aunt, they became suspicious. Although the letters were signed with Kate's name, they were not written in Kate's handwriting. Kate's nieces took the letters, samples of Kate's handwriting, and their account of James' strange activities to the police, who began to investigate.

All of the pieces fell into place. Witnesses could account for everything: the purchase of the quicklime and rope; hiring a moving company to move a heavy trunk from the apartment building and load onto a rented boat; even the questions about the deepest part of the lake for fishing. When Mahoney was picked up for questioning, he was washing Kate's car and had some of her diamonds in his pockets.

When James was arrested in May, there was not enough evidence without Kate's body to hold him for murder—but there was plenty to hold him for forgery. Meanwhile, the police stepped up their search for Kate's body, and on August 8, 1921, they found the trunk. The rope tying it to the lake's floor was mysteriously disturbed, and the trunk had floated to the surface and was rescued by a tugboat.

An autopsy showed that Kate's body contained traces of morphine. James had drugged her, stuffed her into the trunk while still alive, clubbed her over the head, covered her in quicklime, sealed the trunk, and then dropped it in the lake. It is believed that Kate remained alive during the whole ordeal.

James was arrested on the charge of first degree murder on August 10, 1921, with his trial beginning on September 20. More than sixty witnesses took the stand during the trial, which lasted less than two weeks. Lots of information about Mahoney began to surface. Of particular note was his previous crime for which he was on parole when he killed his wife. He had drugged and robbed a young man. Also of interest was the fact that Mahoney was a bigamist. More interestingly, his first wife had left him because he was dealing opium and had tried to kill her.

Mahoney was convicted of first-degree murder and sentenced to be hanged at Walla Walla on December 1, 1922.

James ate his last meal on Thanksgiving, November 30, and was hanged by the neck at 7:02 a.m. on Friday, December 1, 1922. Approximately twelve minutes later, his body was removed from the noose. To the surprise of those witnessing the execution, there were no marks from the ropes on his body.

Could it be Kate's spirit who led authorities to the trunk containing her body? If her body had not been found, James would have gotten away with murder. Did she also have something to do with the odd findings after his hanging?

It seems that Kate could still be around today. Folks living in the Sophie Apartment building where they believe the murder took place have been awakened in the middle of the night by sounds of a woman screaming and running down the hall. When investigated, there are no signs of any trouble. Some say they have felt her as a quick breeze passing, as if someone ran by the apartment. Is it possible that this could be Kate trying to escape from her killer that terrible night?

DENNY PARK

100 Dexter Avenue N

In what appears to be a quaint little park lies the roots of disturbing history. This ground is the very spot upon which stood the Seattle Cemetery. Yes, Denny Park began as one of the city's first official municipal cemeteries. The land was owned by David Denny of the Denny pioneers. In 1861, Denny agreed to take bodies on the land and consolidate graves from smaller, informal cemeteries around the area because of the great demand for space. This agreement lasted until 1884, with a total of 223 burials on the property. It was then decided to donate the land to the city of Seattle to

DENNY PARK

be converted into a city park. But city officials needed to decide what should be done with the high volume of bodies on the site.

O. C. Shorey was in charge of exhuming and re-interring all of the bodies. Half way through the project, problems began. There were many unmarked graves due to a fire that had burned over the cemetery a few years earlier. This fire destroyed many of the wooden markers. Because of these problems, Shorey was worried that he would not be able to find and remove all of the bodies.

Most bodies where moved to the Masonic Cemetery, now known as Lake View Cemetery. Shortly after the Great Seattle Fire of 1889, the city began the regrade of Denny Hill by lowering the land sixty feet. To their surprise, they uncovered graves that Shorey had indeed missed. Due to the sensitive nature of this issue, the remaining bodies were moved in the middle of the night.

In the 1890s the park was named The Seattle Park but later became known as Denny Park. Then by 1930 it became the park you see today. Some claims that a few spirits still linger in their old burial ground, from old pioneers to Native Americans. This could be due to the desecration; the spirits could be looking for their burial sites. Or there may still be a body or two lying beneath its scared ground.

See also: Mother Damnable in Pioneer Square

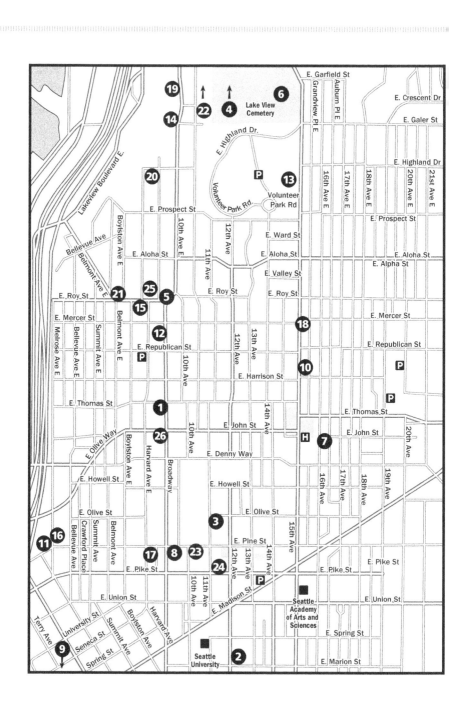

7. CAPITOL HILL

Known among locals as The Hill, Capitol Hill was formerly Broadway Hill. Its current name was given by James A. Moore in 1901. Moore changed the name for two reasons: to please his wife, naming it after her hometown, and in hopes that the state capital would be built on this land. This neighborhood is a hub of coffee shops, art galleries, bars, and Seattle's artistic community. With a diverse population, Capitol Hill contains some of Seattle's wealthiest districts, including "Millionaire's Row," as well as a large population of homeless people and starving artists. Capitol Hill is home to a number of beautiful parks, including Volunteer Park and its historical treasure, Lake View Cemetery.

MAP MARKERS

1. Charlie's Restaurant
2. Photographic Center Northwest
3. Richard Hugo House
4. Grand Army of the Republic Cemetery
5. Harvard Exit Theatre
6. Lake View Cemetery
7. Methodist Church
8. The Burnley School of Professional Art
9. Sorrento Hotel
10. Fifteenth Avenue Video
11. The Baltic Room
12. QFC Broadway Market
13. Volunteer Park
14. Cornish School of Arts
15. D.A.R. Building
16. The Chapel Bar
17. The Egyptian Theater
18. Canterbury Ale & Eats
19. Leary Mansion
20. Scottish Rite of Freemasonry
21. Kerry Hall
22. Seattle Preparatory School
23. Odd Fellows Temple
24. Annex Theatre
25. Loveless Building
26. Bonney-Watson Funeral Home

CHARLIE'S RESTAURANT
217 Broadway E

This cozy restaurant sits on Broadway, Capitol Hill's busiest street. It started out as a furniture showroom in 1914, with its rich dark woods and stained glass windows. These elements create a very pleasant, homey environment for a sit-down meal. Well-known restaurant owner Chuck Quinn, also known as Charlie, opened it as a restaurant opened in 1976.

Patsy Clark's of Spokane, Washington, was another popular restaurant Charlie owned. This 1897 historic mansion, once owned by the Clark family, was converted into a restaurant by Charlie in 1982. Although it was rumored that the place was haunted, these rumors did not stop Charlie from pursuing his dream.

Patsy Clark's is one of Spokane's most-documented haunted hot spots, with strange tales of activities in the wine cellar in the basement—unseen forces throw bottles across the room. Some have even seen the outlines of figures wandering the building. In 1995 the old mansion was sold and has now been converted into offices.

CHARLIE'S RESTAURANT

Charlie's restaurant on Broadway has had its share of hauntings as well. Most encounters have taken place in the back bar. Some have felt cold spots, heard strange sounds, and things have been known to be moved or completely disappear. Are ghosts hanging out at the old furniture store? Spending an evening at Charlie's might help you decide.

PHOTOGRAPHIC CENTER NORTHWEST
900 Twelfth Avenue

Photographic Center Northwest is a school and community arts center dedicated to fine art and documentary photography. Students have witnessed odd things happen here. Some have seen a dark figure roaming the floors. Lights appear to turn off and on without anyone near the controls. But most often they hear footsteps, almost as though someone is following them around the building. Generally, the sound of footsteps emanates from upstairs, as if someone is roaming around on the second floor. Strangely enough, whenever the sound is investigated, no one is up there.

PHOTOGRAPHIC CENTER NORTHWEST

RICHARD HUGO HOUSE
1634 Eleventh Avenue

This old Victorian home, once a funeral home, was originally built in 1902. It now acts as a community center and theater for literary artists. Founded in 1997, the center honors Richard Hugo, who was a Seattle poet and creative writer in the 1960s and 1970s.

It first was Manning's Mortuary, and then it was sold to Bonney-Watson Mortuary and Funeral Home. After that, it was owned by a company called New City Theater, which produced shows. When Hugo House took over the building, staffers realized right away that they had an old funeral home in their possession. They found evidence of this in the basement including a child's coffin. It was soon after they got settled in that odd things started to happen—for example, things being moved around and lights going off. People also began hearing voices and seeing apparitions. An AGHOST investigation picked up sound recordings, including responses to these questions: "Can you tell us your name?" The response was "Yes," and "Can I take your picture?" "Don't" was picked up in what sounds like an older woman's voice.

RICHARD HUGO HOUSE

GRAND ARMY OF THE REPUBLIC CEMETERY

1200 E Howe Street

Just north of Lake View Cemetery sits a small, almost unknown area established in 1895 for the Civil War heroes. This resting place was maintained by G.A.R. until 1922. It was then turned over to the Lake View Cemetery and had 526 graves to tend. Due to land-ownership confusion, the cemetery fell into disrepair throughout the 1940s and 1950s, but the headcount remained when the cemetery was transcribed in 1979. Somehow during the ten years between 1979 and 1989, up to eighteen tombstones went missing, as the cemetery was once again mapped out. Some may have been some stolen before the 1979 transcribing. Also, six burial sites are marked as unknowns. In efforts to clean things up, all of the tombstones were moved to a central location, leaving the bodies where they originally rested but without their markers.

Folks have reported seeing men roaming the grounds dressed in Civil War attire. Passersby and nearby residents have also reported seeing strange lights hovering around the grounds. Some report hearing voices as well as a bugle playing late into the night. Now, thanks to Friends of G.A.R, the cemetery is in good hands and well maintained. Hopefully, this will put the spirits here at rest.

GRAND ARMY OF THE REPUBLIC CEMETERY

HARVARD ExiT THEATRE
807 East Roy Street

One of Seattle's most documented haunted hot spots has been featured in media around the world. This 1925 building was built for the Women's Century Club. At one time Bertha Landes served as the national president and was Seattle's first female mayor in 1926. It is believed that her spirit roams the halls of this theater.

Third Floor: This is believed to be the most active area. People have seen toilets flush on their own in the women's bathroom Once an employee was asked to look in on a gentleman's wife who had been in the bathroom a little longer than expected. The employee did and found the woman fixing herself in the mirror. She told the woman that her husband was waiting outside for her. The woman nodded yes, and the employee stepped back out to let him know that his wife would be right out. But to her

HARVARD EXIT THEATRE

surprise, he was already with his wife, who had been using the second-floor bathroom. The employee then stepped back into the bathroom to find it completely empty.

Another story tells of a manger who had stayed late closing down the building. As he went around the building making sure all the doors were pulled shut, he came to the exit door off the third-floor fire escape. As he pulled the door closed he felt someone pull it back open. Startled, he began playing tug of war with someone on the other side. Finally, after about fifteen seconds of this, he overpowered his opponent and got the door firmly closed. It took a few moments for him to calm down, but then he realized that he should make sure the intruder was off the fire escape. He then pushed open the door to find no one in sight. He thought he would at least hear the person going down the metal staircase, but after examining the door he discovered another oddity. The door didn't even have a handle on the outside, making it impossible for anyone to pull the door back.

Second Floor: This is where the old apartments for abused and needy women were located. These units are no longer used for the living; most of them are just storage space packed with old movie junk. Many of the employees have heard the sounds of dishes being washed or even dropped, and furniture moving across the floors. In the women's bathroom there is a stall whose door will shut and lock on its own. It seems employees are used to having to crawl under the stall door to unlock it.

Main Floor: Many reports here have been focused on the lobby. On occasion the theater would light fires in the old fireplace. One night after putting out the fire, the manger was shocked to find the fire going strong the next morning when he opened for the day. What made the situation even stranger was that the chairs in the lobby had been moved to form a conversation circle, as if a meeting of the women had taken place during the night. A few employees have walked into the lobby to find a woman sitting in one of armchairs; when approached she turns and vanishes. Throughout the main floor people have seen women dressed in turn-of-the-century clothing, which indicates the old members of the women's club still come together for their late-night meetings.

The Basement: This is one area employees refuse to go to alone. They claim there is a very heavy presence lurking in this unmanaged space. Odd noises can be heard, and dark shadows are seen floating across the rooms.

Whatever is going on at the Harvard Exit Theatre, it might be a good place for ghost hunters and ghost enthusiasts to glimpse a lingering past.

See also: Smith Tower in Pioneer Square

LAKE VIEW CEMETERY

1554 Fifteenth Avenue E

Lake View Cemetery has much to offer its visitors, but most come to visit with its occupants. Lake View provides the resting place for some of Seattle's more noteworthy residents. With a rich assortment from Seattle's pioneer past, a sampling of those buried here includes: Mother Damnable (see Pioneer Square), Princess Angeline (see

LAKE VIEW CEMETERY

Pike Place Market), and Dr. David "Doc" Maynard (see Pioneer Square). In fact, the cemetery's popularity grew when the "Doc" passed. After his death, his body was laid in state for more then a month until they made a more direct road to the cemetery. Doc had been known throughout Seattle as a drinker, and so it's quite humorous that employees of the cemetery have had to constantly fix old Doc's upright tombstone every year due to it always being as "tipsy" as Doc himself, until they replaced it with a newer one that rests flat with the ground.

Henry Yesler and Lou Graham are also buried here. Mr. Yesler put Seattle on the map with his steam-powered sawmill. But then he almost destroyed the city by embezzling its funds and taking it almost into bankruptcy. No visitor wants to miss the grave of Lou Graham,who started work as a "seamstress" (which in Seattle translates to a lady of the night) and then built and operated the brothel at the corner of Third Avenue South and South Washington Street. She was so successful that she donated close to a quarter-of-a-million dollars to the city schools when she died. How's that for a seamstress?

For those interested in studying the lost art of stonecutting or the history of the pioneers who developed Seattle, highlights include the burial sites of the Boren family, the Denny family, the Terry family, and the Bell family. On the gravestones, visitors may see interesting names like "Melody Choir," "E. Zippy Rivet," or sayings like "The tour stops here," which is on the tombstone of Robert Ferguson, who wrote a book on the history of Lake View Cemetery.

In addition to the rich history and cultural significance of the graves and markings, a visit to Lake View reveals some of the most beautiful natural sights in the area. The cemetery was opened in 1872 as The Seattle Masonic Cemetery, but the name was changed to Lake View Cemetery in 1890. As the highest point in the city, this location has some of the most beautiful views of the surrounding area (which may account for the name change). From here, visitors can see Lake Union, the Cascades, the Olympic Mountains, and Lake Washington.

As the cemetery is still active, some of the occupants are from Seattle's more recent past. The most famous and most visited graves are those of Bruce Lee and his son, Brandon Lee. Bruce Lee was the first Asian superstar—a martial arts master. But he was also convinced he would never live to be an old man. Both father and son died young, with Bruce dying at thirty-two and Brandon at twenty-eight. Both artists died while at the height of their film careers. On both graves, visitors leave an assortment of gifts including: flowers, pinecones, coins, incense, rocks, fruit, toys, jewelry, photos, letters, and greeting cards. Some visitors have broken off chips from the gravestones as souvenirs. Of course, we know you won't do this! It is disrespectful and illegal. And remember: Someone is always watching you!

Many believe there is an energy around Bruce Lee's grave. Psychics claim that he is not at rest, that he has unfinished business, and that he wants to communicate with the people who loved him. Some even believe that his spirit likes to pull pranks on those who visit him. Visitors have had strange images show up in their pictures from around the site. One person had a particularly strange event happen during his visit. While copying some writing from a piece of paper left on Bruce Lee's gravestone, the wind suddenly snatched the paper and carried it a few feet away. After it was retrieved, the wind snatched it up and carried it away again and again. This game lasted through several tries, until the paper disappeared into the sky. Was this Bruce's way of mischievously reminding us that he is still around?

Lee's ghost is not the only spirit roaming this historic cemetery. Some visitors claim to hear footsteps or catch glimpses of apparitions, but the oddest report of all is that of "Buck," who was a beloved cattle horse for eighteen years. Yes, a ghost horse has been seen wondering through Lake View Cemetery. Some folks have not seen Buck, but rather have heard him clomping around on the cement walkways. Buck was a favorite pet, and when he died in 1884 his owner, Irving Wadleigh, made arrangements to have Buck buried beneath an eight-foot shaft monument. After a newspaper article reported on this monument in 1901, locals were furious at the idea of an animal being buried alongside the graves of their families and friends. So the owner was told to move the horse off the cemetery grounds. But, supposedly, the horse was never moved, just the grave marker. It is believed that Irving got his wish and is secretly buried next to his beloved Buck.

Some accounts tell of an elderly man walking around the cemetery in overalls and cap. He always seemed focused on looking for something. Folks have seen him in the northwest section of the cemetery, close to where Nils Jacob Ohm "Dutch Ned" is buried. He spent most of his adult life paying for a beautiful mausoleum that he called his "Little House," which was destroyed due to decay in the 1970s. Is his spirit confused and looking for his last home of rest?

See also: Dutch Ned in Pioneer Square

METHODIST CHURCH

1601 East John Street

The people of the Methodist community built up in 1864 by the Reverend Daniel Bagley, with his wife Susannah and their seventeen-year-old son, Clarence, were the first to travel Military Road from Fort Vancouver to Seattle, in 1865, founding the historic "Brown Church," built at the corner of Second Avenue and Madison Street.

METHODIST CHURCH

Bagley's duties involved much more than preaching and ministering to his congregation. His most memorable achievement may be convincing Arthur Denny that Seattle would benefit more by being the home to a university rather than being the capitol. Bagley was a significant advocate for bringing what was Territorial University (now UW) to Seattle. After the decision to build the school in Seattle, Bagley was made president of the university's board of commissioners. The University Street entrance of the Olympic Four Seasons Hotel bears a commemorative plaque honoring Denny and Bagley and their work to build the university where the hotel now stands. Another mentionable event in Bagley's life includes his defense of the "Mercer Girls"—women who were recruited from other parts of the country to balance out the ratio of males to females in Seattle. Bagley presided over a large meeting at Yesler Hall and spoke in defense of his friend, Asa Mercer. Bagley even presided over the wedding of Mercer and Annie E. Stephens, one of the "Mercer Girls."

The church on East John was built in 1906 and is now used as an office building for the Catalysis Corporation and is believed to still house the spirits of Reverend Bagley and his wife. Stories say that the Reverend will appear on the stairs or in the bell tower in his black shirt and white collar. Many will feel his presence in the air, and when he does show himself he tends to be missing the lower part of his body. But he is not the only ghost of this former church. His wife, Susannah, has been seen in a white dress with a glowing blue light surrounding her. When she asked the startled onlookers the way out, they pointed to the door, only to watch her float up the stairs and out a window. It appears the spirits of the Methodist church still keep a watchful eye on the church they loved in life.

See also: Mount Pleasant Cemetery in Seattle Cemeteries; University of Washington in University District; Martha Washington School and Park in Seattle Parks

THE BURNLEY SCHOOL OF PROFESSIONAL ART

905 East Pine Street

This building was built in 1906 as the Booth Building. The Cornish School of Music moved to this location in 1914 and operated here as a dance studio until 1921 when they opened a new school. In 1946, Edwin and Elise founded Burnley School of Professional Art and started teaching graphic design and illustration classes until the Art Institute took over. Now the building is currently owned and used by neighboring Seattle Community College, and the primary tenant is a dental clinic.

According to students and workers in the building, stories of a ghost have circulated since the 1960s. Many believe that the spirit of a teenage boy haunts this building. There are two popular beliefs as to how the boy may have died. One is that the boy died due to a fight during which he was pushed down the back staircase. The other is that the boy was a student who committed suicide on the back steps. Either way, the tragic event happened on the back staircase of the building.

In and around that time, a medium was called in to help with strange occurrences that plagued people in the building. The medium put on a séance in hopes of contacting the young boy. During this séance, guests were startled to hear a sudden crash of glass in an upstairs bathroom. When they investigated, they discovered a huge rock, far too big to have been thrown by human hands, had come through the third-floor window. The guests returned to the séance to find the medium doing automatic writing, which lead to the guests to investigate the basement, where they found a mysterious hole in which the stone in the bathroom would fit.

Some claim to feel a cold spot on the step where the boy died. Others say you can feel him moving up and down the stairs. But this is not all that seems to happen here in the building. On some days, workers find furniture has been mysteriously rearranged or stacked during the previous night, when no one was in the building. Numerous tales of footsteps, crashing noises, and books being pushed from their shelves have been reported throughout the building, but predominantly on the second and third floors. The spirit of the teenage boy may be angry due to dying at such a young age, and the energy of his anger is the cause of the ghostly occurrences many experience to this day.

See also: Cornish College of the Arts in this section

SORRENTO HOTEL
900 Madison Street

This building dates back to 1909 when it opened its doors as a luxury hotel, but through the years it was used for many other things including military housing,

SORRENTO HOTEL

women's dorms, and office space. Now it's back to its historic beginnings and is believed to be haunted by its past guests and residents.

Most of the activity seems to be focused around the Hunt Bar. It seems ghosts here are in need of a drink, for many guests have seen wine glasses move across the bar or drinks moving around on tables when unattended. Some have felt their presence or even cold spots, or they have heard footsteps that move around the bar area.

More stories come from the fourth floor near room 408, where witnesses have seen an older woman walk the hall and vanish just outside the room. One report is that a guest died in the room on her visit to Seattle for a friend's funeral. Whoever these ghosts might be, this place has seen many guests and events, and maybe they had so much fun here that they just don't want to leave.

FIFTEENTH AVENUE VIDEO

400 Fifteenth Avenue E

Seattle's Fire Department was established by a city charter in 1883. This old firehouse used as Fire Station No. 7 was built 1920, but in 1971 they moved to a bigger

FIFTEENTH AVENUE VIDEO

location. Volunteers would come to the rescue, and it wasn't until after the Great Seattle Fire of 1889 that Seattle decided to get a more professional set up and began hiring professional firefighters. Fire fighting wasn't the safest job and many lives were lost. This may be why people have had strange things happen in this place, which is now a DVD rental store. Some say they have seen the figure of a man standing in the shadows; doors have opened and closed with no one nearby; videos have flown off the shelves; and one employee has seen a man float across the main floor and disappear.

THE BALTIC ROOM
1207 Pine Street

In business for the last sixteen years, the Baltic Room offers dance music for those who love to get their groove on. Back when it was more of a jazz setting, the spirit of a woman would appear in her fancy dress on the balcony and gaze at the piano player. But just as soon as she would disappear, the spirit of a man in a suit would appear very near to where she had just been. Is she being followed by the man who may have killed her? Or does she just miss the man she loved? No one knows what seems to be going on with these two ghosts. In most cases they don't even react to the living people around them, as if they may be trapped in their own spiritual world.

QFC BROADWAY MARKET
523 Broadway E

Formerly known as The Broadway Market, this structure was built in 1928 to house many private shops. In the 1980s a young man died in the upstairs restroom from a drug overdose. Since his death, strange things have been reported. In July of 2004, Quality Food Centers (QFC) took over the market and converted it into a grocery store. During the renovations, construction workers saw tools turn on and off by themselves; things would disappear and then reappear in the strangest places; and odd noises were heard all night long. Some even saw a young man walking around on the second floor. Security guards have been known to pursue him only to have him disappear, never to be found anywhere the store.

QFC BROADWAY MARKET

Volunteer Park

1247 Fifteenth Avenue E

This park has gone by many different names and has been used for many different purposes. It started as forty acres of land purchased for $2,000 in 1876. Its first function was as the Washelli Cemetery in 1885. This was right after the Denny family donated their property known as "The Seattle Cemetery" to the city of Seattle only to have it converted into a park. Most of those bodies where moved here, but that only lasted two years due to a journalist who published an article in the paper stating that he enjoyed his stroll through the Washelli Cemetery. He found himself in deep communication with nature until he stumbled onto a few tombstones and heard a disembodied voice say, "Dispose of the dead elsewhere; this ground is reserved for the enjoyment of the living." Soon after that article was published, the people of Seattle moved the bodies once more to the neighboring property, Lake View Cemetery. Could this have been the inspirational work of a ghost? Once the bodies were removed, it then became "Lake View Park." And in 1901 it finally took the name Volunteer Park.

By 1912, the park developed into a thing of beauty. With its fishponds, flower beds, and sculptures, the park has many pleasurable sites. Don't miss the water tower and conservatory while visiting here.

VOLUNTEER PARK

The Water Tower: Built in 1906 by what some believe to be the bricks from the Great Seattle Fire, this tower has 106 steps to its observation deck and is one of the highest points of Capitol Hill. But if you're looking for more than just a good view, you might find company of the spiritual kind. Many have seen an older man in overalls sitting on one of the benches on the observation deck. Others have felt or heard him follow them down the steps. Rumor has it that a man fell to his death while building the tower.

The Museum: Security guards have been visited by the spirit of a young girl. When reviewing their outside security camera, the guards see the image of a little girl, just staring into the camera, and then she vanishes before their eyes. This tends to happen late in the night. No one knows who she is. One thing's for certain—anyone who has seen her on the monitors, never wants to meet her in person.

Conservatory: Built in 1912 to house a major orchid collection, this building now houses an outstanding display of flowering plants from all areas of the world. But the oddest is by far the titan arum or Amorphophallus titanum, otherwise known as the corpse flower. When this strange plant blooms, its fragrance smells like a decaying corpse.

The rest of the park has its share of ghost stories as well. People have seen apparitions roaming around the grounds. Could these be the souls of bodies that might have been left behind when the cemetery was moved?

CORNISH COLLEGE OF THE ARTS

1501 Tenth Avenue E

Now the Bright Water and Gage Art School, this building was founded as a fine art school in 1914 by pianist and voice teacher Nellie Cornish. Famed faculty, students, and staff include: Mark Tobey, Merce Cunningham, Martha Graham, John Cage, Helmi Juvonen, Peter Meremblum, Berthe Poncy, Ann Wilson (of Heart), Gary Hill, and Brendan Fraser. In 2003 the school moved to a new location in downtown Seattle.

However, it seems they left some of their spirits behind. In the Bright Water portion of the school, a young man apparently fell to his death from a ladder in the old gym. Students have seen and heard him walking along the upstairs walkway. He

CORNISH COLLEGE OF THE ARTS

also plays pranks around the old theater as well: Whenever they have a performance, odd things to happen.

The Gage portion of the school also has its share of ghosts. Students' art supplies disappear and reappear in strange locations or may never show up again. One story is that a student working late alone on a painting stepped away to retrieve more supplies, when he returned to his painting, he was started to find red hand prints all over it. Was this the work of a ghost who wanted to lend a spiritual hand?

D.A.R. BUILDING
800 East Roy Street

The Rainier Chapter House of the D.A.R. (Daughters of the American Revolution) is a replica of George Washington's Mount Vernon home. Opening its doors in 1925, this location served as the venue for many events for the Women's Century Club. It is now more popular as a wedding venue with its beautiful colonial-style heritage.

People report many sounds including: a woman talking when no woman is around, eerie old-time music playing in empty rooms, and other strange noises. On a few occasions, witnesses have seen the apparition of a young female descending the staircase, wearing a gown from the 1800s. Could this be a bride dressed in period costume, reliving her wedding day? Or someone from the mid 1900s wearing her mother's old wedding dress?

D.A.R. BUILDING

THE CHAPEL BAR

THE CHAPEL BAR

1600 Melrose Avenue

Built in 1922 as the E.R. Butterworth & Sons Mortuary, the business was carried on by five generations of the Butterworth family, and they operated at this location until 2000, when they sold the building, which was converted into offices. Butterworth's relocated to another facility on Queen Anne.

It now is home to a high-profile bar known as The Chapel Bar, which moved in in 2003 next to attorneys' offices. However, the bar still has its funeral-home style. In fact, the new owners designed the bar to maintain its "deathly" historic charm. The bar itself is made from the cremation vaults that were housed in the basement. If you study them, you may even find the identification numbers or even a name or two. In fact, this is where Bruce and Brandon Lee's funeral services were held.

Many claim that among the bottled spirits are the spirits of people's dead loved ones. Employees and customers have seen and heard some of the strangest things throughout the night. Pictures taken in the bar also reveal things that cannot be explained. Many have seen ghostly figures in the mirrors and a woman on the upper balcony above the entrance. Former employees have also reported witnessing a glass fly straight up in the air and then crashing down onto the dishwasher in the bar.

In 2010 AGHOST investigated this site and found it to be very active that night. Here psychics picked up on the woman in the balcony and the name "Robert." When asked to give a sign that the spirits were present, the bar's speaker system kicked on with a loud and disturbing static sound that lasted for at least ten minutes. Soon after that, banging sounds where heard. The Chapel Bar is open late into the witching hour, so go find out for yourself what's going on.

See also: Butterworth's in Pike Place Market; Lake View Cemetery in Capitol Hill

THE EGYPTIAN THEATRE
805 East Pine Street

Housed in an old Masonic temple built in 1915, the Egyptian Theatre got its start as the Moore Theatre in Belltown. Two young Canadians leased the Moore, and, with some Egyptian designs painted around the entrance, opened the Moore Egyptian Theater in 1975. When their lease ran out, they turned to Capitol Hill for their next venue, stripping the Moore down and transferring the Egyptian art to its nownew found home. This single-screen theater is one of many historic sites owned by Landmark Theatres. In the early 1980s it became the home of the Seattle International Film Festival, the largest festival in North America.

THE EGYPTIAN THEATRE

Today, witnesses see a dark figure roaming the theater aisles after the last showing. The figure is described as a large, possibly caped and hooded black mass. Could this be a deceased member of the old Masonic lodge who wore a hooded robe in a ceremony?

CANTERBURY ALE & EATS

534 Fifteenth Avenue E

Walking into this tavern is like stepping back in time. With its wooden paneling, mounted antlers, and fireplace, Canterbury Ale & Eats looks more like an old medieval tavern than a modern pub. In 1978, a man was shot in the face during a bar fight. No one knows who started the fight or why, but the tragic event took place near the fireplace, where the man eventually died. Folks accustomed to the ghost living in the tavern say that he can be seen in the mirror closest to the fireplace. If you look in the mirror, you will soon see a strange man looking down at the ground in the reflection— but this man is nowhere in the bar. They also say that if you look at him long enough, he will eventually begin to look up at you, only to show you that he has no face.

Late one night, a bartender was closing up. He shut down the jukebox and went on to finish his other closing-time duties. Naturally, he was surprised to hear the jukebox switch on all by itself. The strangest thing, though, was the song it played—"The End" by the Beatles. Others swear they have seen the dark figure of a man wander though the bar only to vanish in front of their eyes.

After hearing these stories, it's hard not to believe that the past still haunts this tavern. Could this ghost be looking for his killer?

LEARY MANSION
1551 Tenth Avenue E

This lovely mansion was built in 1903 and replicates a house the Learys fell in love with while in Ireland on their honeymoon. Unfortunately John Leary passed before their dream house was completed, leaving his wife, Eliza, alone with the huge estate. After she died, the property was sold to the Olympia Diocese.

In 1987 an arsonist set fire to the house destroying a major portion of this fine building. Shortly after it was restored, strange things started to happen: the sounds of furniture moving around and the sounds of walking in the attic space. Lights would turn on all on their own when someone entered a room, as if to greet the person. For a party, employees had obtained permission to use one of Mrs. Leary's dresses on

LEARY MANSION

a mannequin for display. One employee thought it would be fun to set the dressed figure in front of a mirror in Mrs. Leary's old dressing room to provide an eerie scene for those who would happen to look in. But after a while, they decided to move the mannequin out to the front stairs for all the visitors to see. Shortly after that, the mannequin disappeared and was found back in the old dressing room. The weird thing is no one knows how it got back there. They think maybe Mrs. Leary didn't like her dress on display. One person even claims they may have seen Mrs. Leary herself walking across the lobby in a long gown.

If you take the tour of the building, you may recognize some of the interior—if you have seen the Stephen King movie *Red Rose*. They used the lobby for Rose's bedroom and the stairway where they hung Rose's portrait. During filming, the crew experienced their share off oddities. One crew member didn't believe folks when they blamed the strange happenings on the ghost rumored to haunt the building, and he would constantly joke and mock the spirits. On the last day of filming, he stepped into the restroom and, to his surprise, found himself locked in from the inside. It took fifteen minutes to finally get him out, and he left more open-minded to the idea that something paranormal had just happened.

For you fans of the movie *Rose Red*, Thornewood Castle in Lakewood, Washington, just forty minutes out of Seattle, was used for the exterior shots.

SCOTTISH RITE OF FREEMASONRY

On the corner of Harvard and Highland

Unfortunately, this building no longer stands. It was replaced by townhouse condominiums in 2006. Lost forever, but maybe not forgotten, this building was believed to be haunted by a mysterious knocking. On many occasions, members would hear a strange knocking. For years they tried to figure out the cause of the sound, even hiring professionals to investigate. The source of the knocking was never found, but it appeared to have intelligence. The knocking would answer yes or no questions with one knock for yes and two knocks for no. It would also repeat certain patterns or rhythms. So is this knocking ghost gone for good? Maybe not—residents may discover a strange knocking sound in their new condos. Happy housewarming!

SCOTTISH RITE OF FREEMASONRY

KERRY HALL

710 East Roy

Built in 1921 for The Cornish School of Arts and named after longtime school patron, Mrs. Olive Kerry, this building is the last of the original school structures still standing after the school moved to a downtown location.

Students have always felt a presence within its halls. One story claims that a teacher stayed late one night to help a student with a paper. As he waited for the student to arrive, he decided to grade some papers. While doing so, someone came up behind him and started to massage his shoulders. He thanked the helping hands only to find no one behind him. The frightened teacher ran from his office only to find the student he had been waiting for just outside his office door.

KERRY HALL

SEATTLE PREPARATORY SCHOOL

2400 Eleventh Avenue E

Seattle Preparatory School is a private Jesuit high school founded in 1891. By 1919 the school settled in its current location, but where the school stands today used to be a cemetery known as the Holy Cross Cemetery. Purchased in 1884, the land became a two-acre cemetery plot in 1885, the same year the first burials were made. As it was becoming too wet for burial ground, the cemetery was rarely used and had only accumulated up to one hundred bodies. By 1893 the land was ordered vacated, and the cemetery was closed. In 1905 all of the bodies were moved to Calvary Cemetery.

Students have had a number of strange things happen while on campus. Many have seen apparitions wandering through the halls. Lights flicker when students mock the spirits. In the girls' locker room, locker doors slam on their own and things disappear from lockers.

The library may have some ghostly activity of its own. Here students and staff have seen books fly off shelves and dark figures standing in the aisles that disappear when looked at directly.

Could these be the ghosts of the bodies left behind when the old cemetery moved?

See also: Cavalry Cemetery in Seattle Cemeteries

ODD FELLOWS TEMPLE
919 East Pine Street E

The history of the Odd Fellows is fascinating. The basic idea was to create a fraternal organization for members of different trades, unlike the guilds that were made up of the same. All the members of a guild worked at the same trade like the Bakers and the Brewers, but the Odd Fellows came from various disciplines. The purpose of the Fellowship is charity.

Founded in England in the seventeenth century, the Odd Fellows migrated to the United States in 1819. Odd Fellowship in Seattle dates from August 1870 when C.C. Hewitt instituted Olive Branch No. 4 with a handful of members. Membership grew quickly, and another lodge was started. In June 1876 H.R. Struve instituted Seattle Lodge No. 7. With two lodges in Seattle, members applied to set up an encampment. On August 24, 1877, Unity Encampment No. 2 was chartered. Membership continued to grow, and by 1892, there were eight Odd Fellow organizations in Seattle.

The decision to build the Odd Fellows Temple was made due to the rapid and continued growth of the Odd Fellows through the early part of the twentieth century. In 1907 Olive Branch No. 4, Seattle No. 7, Germania No. 102, Golden Link No. 150, and Anchor No. 221 began construction of the Beaux Arts/American Renaissance-style building, which is one of the largest lodges on the West Coast. Occupation of the building began in June of 1909.

The building is quite large, with three great halls. Inside two of these halls stand proscenium stages, which is the reason why so many arts organizations have taken residence in this building through the years. Along with the secrecy of the Odd Fellows, perhaps the mysteries of the theater have conjured up some ghosts in this enormous property.

Today, many who have been inside the old theater have had the feeling of somebody watching them, even when they are completely alone. Some have heard old-time music playing inside when walking by the theater only to find it stop when they opened the doors. One person walked in on a 1920s party, just in time to see all its guests vanish within seconds of each other. Was there a party that somehow got captured within the walls of the old temple? And if so, whose party was it?

ANNEX THEATRE
1100 East Pike Street

In what houses the theater today was once an auto shop garage built in the early 1900s. People believe that a mechanic was found dead under a car while working here. This could be why many folks who work in the theater have seen a man in a blue-and-white jumper wandering the grounds and vanishing before they can get a good look at him. Also, the staff has had trouble with stage lights going on and off, apparently controlled by unseen forces. A shadowy figure hangs out in the control booth, and items turn up missing only to be found in the oddest places. Many are frightened by this male's presence, and some have even given him the nickname "Frank." But during a late-night séance with some of the staff, it seems the name "Robert" was spelled out by the ghost.

LOVELESS BUILDING

LOVELESS BUILDING
806 East Roy Street

Constructed in 1930 and known as the Studio Building, this structure was developed for Seattle artists to live and work in. The designer, Arthur L. Loveless, was famed for his distinct Tudor Revivalist style. Some well-known artists who lived here include photographers Ella E. McBride and Myra Albert Wiggins—plus Arthur Loveless himself.

Now with coffee shops and other businesses surrounding it, many working or living here have felt the presence of an unseen force. Some think it could be Arthur himself, who died in 1971. An older male spirit has been seen wandering through the building, and strange noises have been heard. Doors open without assistance, and on a few occasions employees heard a radio turned up when no one was around to do it.

BONNEY-WATSON FUNERAL HOME
Southwest Corner of East Olive and Broadway E

Bonney-Watson began serving the Seattle area in 1868, making the funeral home the oldest in the Pacific Northwest. However, the company's name changed several times along the way and did not become Bonney-Watson until 1903. The history of the company begins in the 1850s, when the Bonney family settled in the Puget Sound area.

The Bonney family had many daughters, known as the "beautiful Bonney girls." In 1860 Oliver South Shorey married Mary Bonney, one of the "girls." In 1861 they moved to Seattle where Shorey began his trade as a cabinetmaker. In addition to his work making and selling furniture, Shorey helped to build Rev. Daniel Bagley's Territorial University (known today as the University of Washington). Rev. Bagley spearheaded the idea to build the large university, and Shorey helped build it. His hands touched the four columns, L I F E. These columns remain standing on the university location. After helping to build Territorial University, Shorey opened a cabinet shop on Third and Cherry Streets. He soon added to his business the task of building coffins, as was often the case with cabinetmakers. Building coffins led to taking part in the undertaking business. By 1881 his brother-in-law, L.W. Bonney, moved to Seattle and became a partner in the business. As the city was growing, there were more people dying and more work for the business. Shorey-Bonney operated until the Great Seattle Fire of 1889.

Haunting Fact

EVP (Electronic Voice Phenomena) is when voices of the dead or other sounds can be heard on a recorder (such as analog tape, digital, and video recorders) that should not have been recorded. These voices have been known to answer questions, make comments on what is going on at the time or of past events. Only when the recording is played back can the EVPs be heard. Investigators are still looking into how EVPs happen. One thing is for sure—it's one of the simplest ways to determine if a location may be haunted.

After the fire, Shorey sold his share of the business to G.M. Stewart and moved on to other interests. Many documents were destroyed in the Great Fire, but Shorey's records before and after the event remain important for historians.

Bonney partnered with Stewart until 1903, when his shares were sold to the sexton of Lake View Cemetery, Harry W. Watson. From 1903 until the present, the sign of the business reads Bonney-Watson. The business still remains in the family and is Seattle's oldest business establishment.

The location of the business has changed through the years. From 1906 until 1912, the company was housed where the Seattle Tower now stands. In 1912 Bonney-Watson moved to Olive and Broadway, but that building was eventually sold to Seattle Community College. Many students during that time talked about the spirits that haunted it, including feeling the chills and hearing disembodied feet walking the grounds. The building has long been torn down, and the lot now hosts a new building for U.S. Bank.

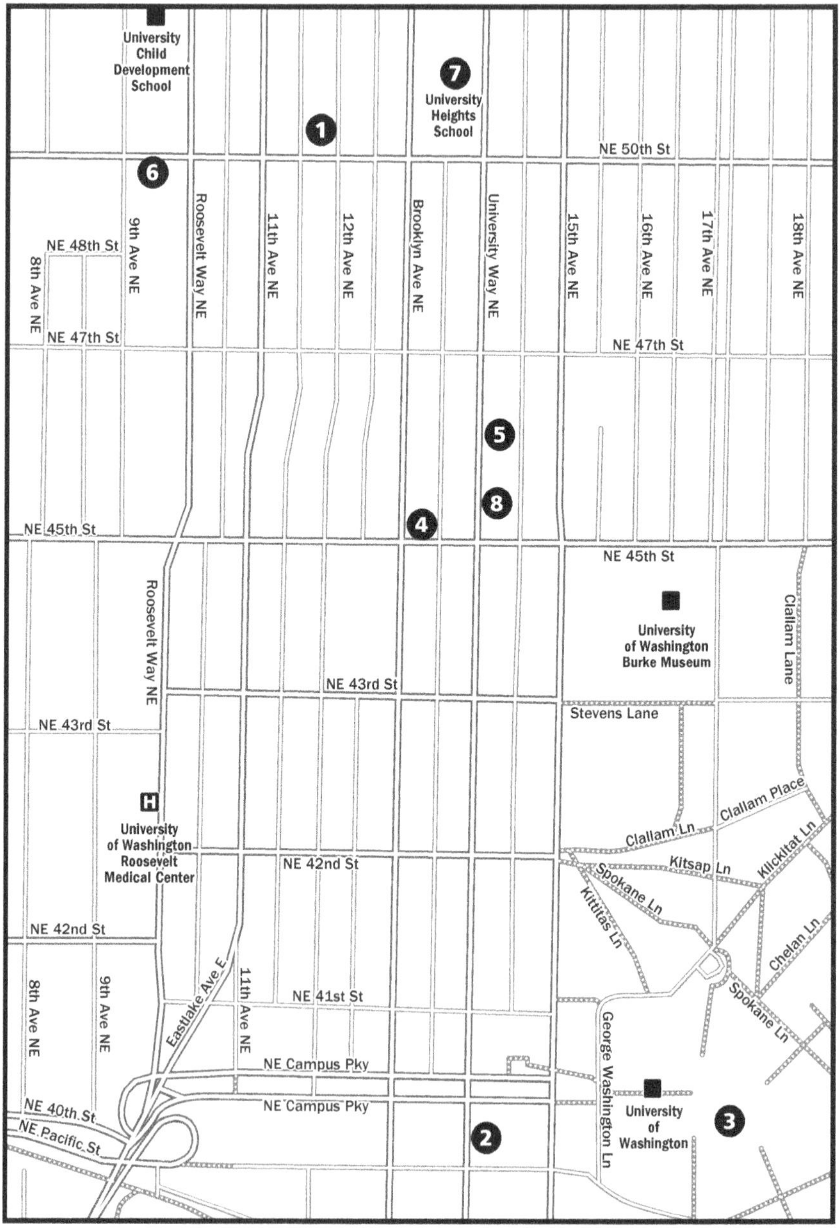

University Child Development School

1

7
University Heights School

6

NE 50th St

8th Ave NE

9th Ave NE

Roosevelt Way NE

11th Ave NE

12th Ave NE

Brooklyn Ave NE

University Way NE

15th Ave NE

16th Ave NE

17th Ave NE

18th Ave NE

NE 48th St

NE 47th St

NE 47th St

5

8

4

NE 45th St

NE 45th St

University of Washington Burke Museum

Clallam Lane

NE 43rd St

Stevens Lane

Roosevelt Way NE

NE 43rd St

Clallam Place

Clallam Ln

Clallam Ln

Kitsap Ln

Klickitat Ln

H
University of Washington Roosevelt Medical Center

NE 42nd St

Spokane Ln

Kittitas Ln

Chelan Ln

NE 42nd St

8th Ave NE

9th Ave NE

Eastlake Ave E

11th Ave NE

NE 41st St

Spokane Ln

NE Campus Pky

NE Campus Pky

George Washington Ln

University of Washington

3

NE 40th St

NE Pacific St

2

8. UNIVERSITY DISTRICT

This area is known as University District because it's the home of the University of Washington's main campus and the University of Washington (UW). The Avenue, the unofficial name of University Way N.E., is the heart of the University District. With its coffee shops and trendy food joints, this serves as a meeting place for university students as it struggles with economic growth. One of the trademarks of this area is the "Avenue Rats," the transient and homeless youth of Seattle. Some of the highlights of this area are the annual May U District Street Fair and coffee shops and bookstores with late hours.

MAP MARKERS

1. YMCA
2. College Inn Pub
3. University of Washington
4. The Neptune Theatre
5. Gargoyles Statuary
6. Seven Gables Theatre
7. University Heights Building
8. Wells Fargo Bank

YMCA

5003 Twelfth Avenue NE

Seattle YMCA (Young Men's Christian Association) was organized on August 7, 1876 to help build strong kids, strong families, and a strong community. Today, the organization is made up of twelve branches, two resident camps, and more than 630 programs throughout the community. The University Family YMCA building, built in 1951, has a few spirits volunteering their time for a good cause. The basement workout room has paranormal activity that is more active at night when everyone has gone home for the day. Night janitors have heard voices and footsteps coming from upstairs when they know they are the only ones in the building. There may be something lingering in the furnace room. As to who or what, you may have to find out for yourself.

YMCA

COLLEGE INN PUB

4000 University Way NE

This location was the former Ye College Inn, positioned across the street from the University. In addition to the pub and the twenty-seven guest rooms, the building houses a café, a convenience store, and a coffee shop.

The University of Washington moved to its current location in 1895. At that time, the school was isolated from much of the city. To remedy this, and to commemorate the Gold Rush to the Yukon through Alaska, the city's entrepreneurs decided to hold an exhibition, known as the Alaska-Yukon Expedition.

Charles Cowen, an Englishman, had moved to Seattle in 1900. In 1906 he purchased a large portion of land near the campus. He developed much of this land and commissioned Graham and Myers to erect Ye Old College Inn in 1909. The building opened on June 6, 1909 just in time for the Expedition. Designed in the Tudor Revival Style, the Inn attracted visitors looking for comfortable accommodations without extravagance.

In 1916, the business changed its name to The College Hotel. This confused some, leading many to refer to the building as The College Inn Hotel. Many businesses populated the ground floors through the years, including dressmakers, cigar shops, and dining establishments.

COLLEGE INN & PUB

Prohibition came and went, but the city had a two-mile dry rule surrounding the campus. The campus remained dry until 1969, but the building did not hold a tavern until 1973.

Today, the entrance into the subterranean pub is a few feet from the sidewalk, down a small alley. Patrons descend a flight of stairs to gain entrance, but once inside, they enjoy all of the comforts of a neighborhood pub. Quite large inside, the pub has working fireplaces with fireside chairs, pool tables, dartboards, and a jukebox.

Employees and guests have seen an Irish man in a khaki trench coat lingering in the back room. Story has it that this could be the spirit of Howard Bok, a sailor in search of gold when he was killed in one of the rooms in the inn. Beer mugs move on their own, and shadowy hands appear along the bar as if waiting for a drink to slide on by.

In the inn, many guests have reported seeing apparitions in the rooms and walking down the halls. Some have smelled perfumes from unknown locations. Guests return to their rooms to find them disrupted. Toilets flush in the middle of the night for no reason.

UNIVERSITY OF WASHINGTON
1400 NE Campus Parkway

Opened in November of 1861 as the Territorial University of Washington, the University of Washington (UW) is the largest university in the Pacific Northwest. UW has three campuses, with the largest making up the University District neighborhood of Seattle. The two smaller campuses are located in Tacoma and Bothell. In its history, UW has closed three times for lack of funds and/or students. In fact, it took the college twenty-five years for its first student to ever graduate—Clara A. McCarty in 1876. Today, UW is ranked highly among universities in the United States. UW has had many lives, openings and closings, but also various locations. Its former haunt is present-day Metropolitan Tract. The university continues to own this property. Originally, the board wanted to sell this land when moving to its present location, but it proved fortuitous to keep the grounds. Renting out the property generates millions of dollars for the university each year.

UNIVERSITY OF WASHINGTON QUAD

Not much remains from the original campus. The Fairmont Olympic Hotel stands on the grounds of the main building. The only trace of the original campus is four large white columns known as LIFE. Each of the pillars is thought to represent one of the following: (L)oyalty, (I)ndustry, (F)aith, (E)fficency. These pillars stand near the Sylvan Grand Theatre and are thought to be haunted. Supposedly, if you venture here at night, the trees and shrubs shake violently to scare you off. You may even hear the growls of a large animal. Some have even seen the spirit of a young man dressed in dark clothes, walking through the columns only to vanish on the other side. The story is different if you come during the day. Many feel a more pleasant, comforting spirit, believed to be Professor Edmond Meany who fought to preserve the columns from the original site in 1910.

University District holds the main campus of UW, settled near Portage and Union Bays with beautiful views of the surrounding natural world: mountains, lakes, and cherry blossoms. The campus is made up of a large number of buildings, the oldest of which is Denny Hall. Built in 1895, this building was named for pioneer Arthur

Denny. Denny Hall served as the administration building when the university moved in the same year.

Since its migration to its new location, the University has had steady growth. UW's current student body is roughly forty-three thousand. Home to military personnel during both World Wars, the campus was equally populated with students protesting during the 1960s and 70s. The branch campuses of Tacoma and Bothell were added in the 1990s.

Many students have roamed the halls and lived in the dormitories of the school, but the most infamous must be serial killer Ted Bundy, who graduated from UW in 1972, shortly before he began his rampage. Those who knew Bundy noticed a remarkable change in his personality and behavior during his years at UW. Who knows what dark changes happened to him while he slept in his gray dormitory or stumbled through his classes in psychology?

There are other stories of the creepy and the strange on campus. Here are a few to look into when you visit the school.

Suzzallo Library, named after President Henry Suzzallo, first opened in 1927 and was referred to as "the soul of the university." Suzzallo believed the library should be a monumental cathedral-like building dominating the entire campus architecturally, which it does to this day. This beautiful gothic building also has the ghost of a young woman in a raincoat and galoshes. She only appears on rainy nights in the fall and winter months. She can be seen walking in and heading up the grand staircase, obviously dripping wet, but surprisingly she leaves no evidence, not even a wet footprint.

In the ceramics and metal arts building, students have seen faucets turn on and off on their own—the pottery wheels will do the same. In the senior studio, one student had the most bizarre experience. When entering the building early one morning, he saw what he described as various shadows darting around the room disturbing the papers on the walls, before they completely vanished. Another time he turned the lights on in the classroom and stepped out for just a minute to find the lights turned back off when he returned.

THE NEPTUNE THEATRE
1303 NE Forty-fifth Street

This theater dates back to 1921 and stands as one of Seattle's last remaining single-screen theaters. Owned by Landmark Theatres (which owns many of Seattle's historic theaters), this gem was designed to really live up to its name, with renovations such as a snack bar that looks like a ship, completed in 1994.

Here people have named the haunting "the smoking ghost" due to the smells of tobacco when there is clearly no one smoking in the area. In some reports, the smoking ghost follows some employees backstage. They also believe it's the spirit of a man because he tends to flirt with the women by tugging on their hair, pinching their bottoms, and tapping them on their shoulders.

THE NEPTUNE THEATRE

In addition to the smoking ghost, cold spots have been felt, and many have seen the apparition of a woman in the lobby. In fact, a janitor saw a woman in a long, dark gown and addressed her to let her know the theater was closed. As he watched her exit, she did not walk but floated across the floor five inches off the ground! That's when he knew he was not talking to the living! Many others have reported seeing a woman bathed in white light. She wears a white dress and has long flowing dark hair. Could they be different women? Just how many unearthly beings reside at the Neptune Theatre?

GARGOYLES STATUARY
4550 University Way Northeast

This gothic shop is filled with dragons, ghouls, and, of course, gargoyles. In 1994 this shop of unique relics took over what was once the Unicorn Pub. Shortly after they opened their doors at the new site, trouble began brewing. It seems the ghost that haunted the pub was not going to make things easy for the new owners. The shop started to have small fires, floods, and electrical troubles. It wasn't long before they also noticed a creepy face appearing in a watermark on their ceiling. Could this be the work of a troubled spirit still lingering about?

GARGOYLES STATUARY

SEVEN GABLES THEATRE
911 NE Fiftieth Street

At first glance, you wouldn't think of this as a movie theater. With its cozy home-like appeal, this single-screen theater was built in 1925 and is another theater operated by Landmark since 1989. It was an American Foreign Legion dance hall until 1976, when Seven Gables Theatre's founder, Randy Finley. converted it into the chain's flagship theater and corporate office.

Today, it focuses on independent and foreign language films, but that is not all it has to offer moviegoers. Many have claimed to see shadowy figures and hear strange sounds when things settle down for the evening.

SEVEN GABLES THEATRE

UNIVERSITY HEIGHTS BUILDING

5031 University Way NE

University Heights is a subdivision of the University District neighborhood. Although not often used today, this area's name dates back to 1905. A map from that same year delineates the boundaries of "University Heights" as follows: Brooklyn Avenue to the west, Fifteenth Avenue to the east, Forty-fifth Street to the south, and Fifty-fifth Street to the north.

The building that serves as the University Heights Center for the Community Association (UHCCA) had been the University Heights Elementary School (UHES) for more than eighty-five years when the Seattle School Board decided to close its doors in 1989.

Originally opening its doors in 1902, the school was temporarily known as the Morse School until 1903. UHES operated until 1972 when Alternative School # 2 took possession of more than two thirds of the school's space. When the school closed in 1989, the Alternative School moved to the Decatur School.

Although the building was declared a city landmark in 1977, nothing could stop the school board from closing the school. Residents took up the fight to save the school and achieved a kind of victory: They saved the building, which was converted into a community center.

The University Heights Center for the Community Association was founded in 1989 by residents of the University District neighborhood. How fitting that one of the oldest elementary school buildings in the Pacific Northwest now houses a community center. This center serves as a "heart" for this neighborhood. In addition to the classes and activity hub, the center also serves as a meeting place for organizations throughout the community.

There is a story of a little boy ghost who haunts this site. When it was an elementary school he was locked in a closet and forgotten over the weekend. When they returned he was dead.

Many visitors and workers have witnessed strange happenings: the sounds of someone walking or running on the second floor when no one is up there; doors opening and closing on their own; and shadowy figures roaming the building. On

AGHOST investigations, many recordings of a woman had been captured. The spirit of the woman that haunts this place has also been known to lock and unlock doors.

WELLS FARGO B A N K
4500 University Way NE

It seems that the ghost living in this old bank is obsessed with anything that has to do with water. On the lower floor, bottles of water disappear and show up in odd places; cups of water tip over on their own; the faucets turn on by themselves; and the sound of running water can be heard and yet never is traced to a source. Some believe they have seen the ghost and have described a large, dark figure roaming the halls. It was found that the building was built over a frog pond when the area was in early development. Could something have happened to someone in that pond? Maybe that's why the ghost is so focused on water.

WELLS FARGO BANK

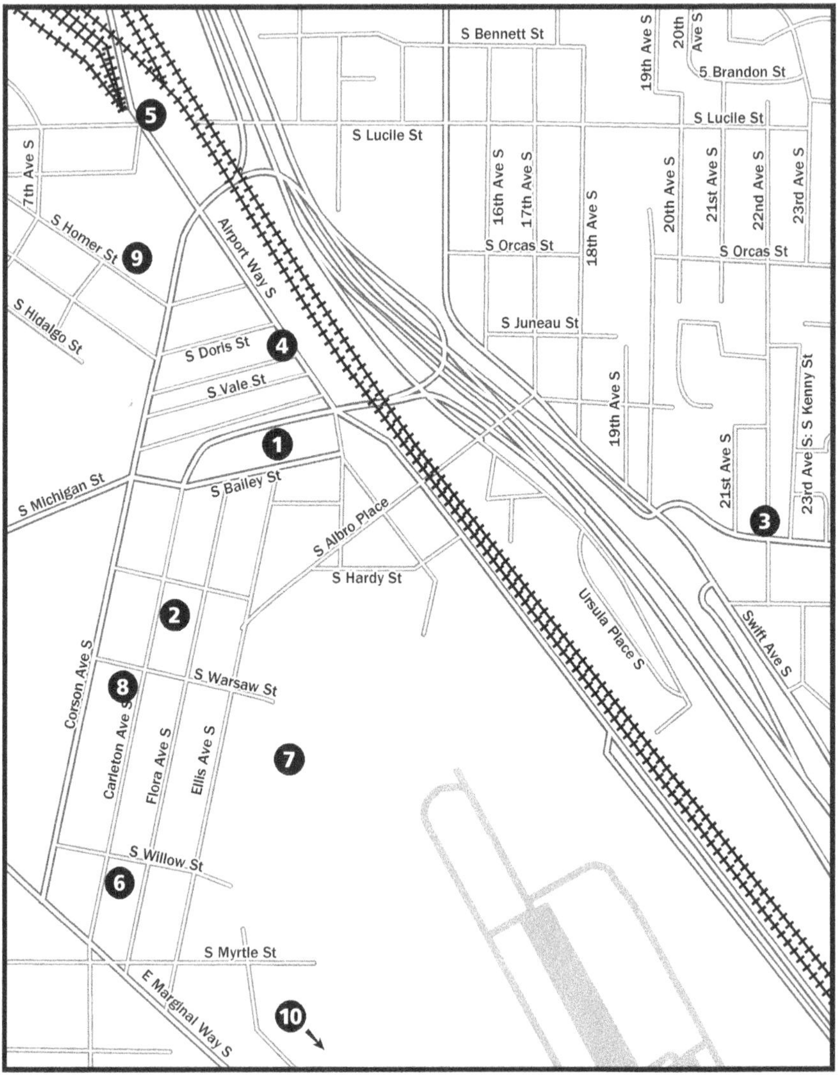

S Bennett St
19th Ave S
20th Ave S
S Brandon St
S Lucile St
S Lucile St
7th Ave S
16th Ave S
17th Ave S
18th Ave S
20th Ave S
21st Ave S
22nd Ave S
23rd Ave S
S Homer St
Airport Way S
S Orcas St
S Orcas St
S Hidalgo St
S Juneau St
S Doris St
S Vale St
19th Ave S
S Kenny St
21st Ave S
23rd Ave S
S Michigan St
S Bailey St
S Albro Place
S Hardy St
Ursula Place S
Swift Ave S
Corson Ave S
S Warsaw St
Carleton Ave S
Flora Ave S
Ellis Ave S
S Willow St
S Myrtle St
E Marginal Way S
1
2
3
4
5
6
7
8
9
10

9. GEORGETOWN

Luther Collins staked his claim here back on September 16, 1851, just before Seattle was founded. Julius Horton named it after his son in 1890. Before Seattle annexed it in 1910, Georgetown existed as an independent city. Part of the residents' resistance to being annexed by Seattle may have had to do with prohibitionism. It seems that this settlement gained popularity when it developed its own red-light district. One of Georgetown's most memorable businesses was Rainier Brewing Company, which began in 1882 and closed in 1999. Today, Georgetown is home to a number of shops and businesses.

MAP MARKERS

1. Central Baptist Church
2. Georgetown Castle
3. Comet Lodge Cemetery
4. Jules Maes Saloon
5. Georgetown Liquor Company
6. Coliman Restaurant
7. Steam Plant
8. Country Inn Roadhouse
9. Georgetown Playfield
10. Museum of Flight

CENTRAL BAPTIST CHURCH

1201 South. Bailey Street

This Korean Baptist church was built in 1927 by the Masons and was a former Masonic temple, which some believe was used to sacrifice animals and perhaps humans. After this building sat vacant for a few years, the Korean Baptist Church took over in the 1980s. It has been reported to have mysterious sounds, slamming doors, and sightings of a strange old man roaming around. It is also rumored to be the dwelling of demonic energies, due to possible odd rituals that may have been practiced there.

It is also believed that some of these hauntings could be caused by the horrible plane crash that happened in 1949 because this area may have been hit with debris from the crash in which many were killed as well.

CENTRAL BAPTIST CHURCH

GEORGETOWN CASTLE

6420 Carleton Avenue

Built in 1902, Georgetown Castle is a three-story, Victorian-era mansion. The castle boasts more than half-a-dozen bedrooms, high turrets, and a wraparound porch, under which may be hidden many of the house's secrets. The castle's original owner, Peter Gessner, made a mint at Pioneer Square's Central Tavern. You name it and he had his hands in it. He ran booze, cards, dice, and women. If there was money to be made at it, Gessner made sure he took his share. With all of this cash, he was flush enough to build a dream house for his young wife—and not just a dream house but a castle!

However, he died living alone in the unfurnished house less than a year later. His mouth was burned with carbolic acid. Some said it was suicide, others suggested not. In any case, his wife, Lizzie, married Peter's business partner, Edward J. Ward, less than five months after Peter's death. Eventually, they moved into the castle, enjoying the house that Peter built.

Through the years, the house has been a private home, a boardinghouse, and a brothel. One of its owners was Dr. Willis Corson in 1912, who occupied it after he retired from the old King County Almshouse and Hospital just three blocks down the street. Many believe that the doctor performed examinations, surgeries, and even secret abortions on the property, which may explain the claims of finding the remains of an infant under the back porch in the late 1950s. Whatever events may have taken place in this house, Georgetown Castle is haunted.

More than one apparition has appeared to visitors, but the two most commonly witnessed are a woman with coal-black eyes and an ominous-looking man. Some believe the man is the woman's killer. He is never far behind her, and she appears to be clutching her throat with one hand and striking the air with another. Perhaps she is reliving the moments before her death as she fought off her killer.

Three possibilities have been offered to identify the woman: Sarah, Gessner's daughter-in-law; a prostitute named Mary Christian or Magdalena; or an unnamed Spanish immigrant. It is believed that, whoever the woman is, she or someone close to her murdered her illegitimate child and buried the dead child under the stairs of the porch. Some stories say the woman was the killer; others say the father or lover killed the child, locked the woman in a room, and she went mad. Whichever story you choose to believe, the ghost is still there.

Another specter is a man named Manny, perhaps Spanish. Manny can be heard and sometimes seen walking up and down the main staircase. An eyewitness to one of Manny's stair climbs also claims that the woman was a prostitute named Magdalena not Sarah, and, in fact, the spirit gets very upset when referred to as Sarah.

Tenants who lived in the building in the 1970s claim to have discovered a walled-up room with a pronounced cold spot. The owners of the house at that time also claimed to have spoken with a female ghost. Whether Magdalena or Sarah, she claimed to have been raped by a man who later killed her baby and buried it under the porch. Sound familiar?

Sights and sounds continue to scare visitors, such as the sounds of a woman or baby crying, or the sounds of children playing and laughing on the third floor. Could this be the children of the women working in the brothel? At one point, so many tenants were freaked out by the unusual occurrences the landlord required they sign a liability waiver when putting down a deposit. One tenant even committed suicide. Perhaps his ghost also walks the halls of the castle.

In 2010 AGHOST filmed an investigation here for the Travel Channel. During that filming the psychic picked up on a strong negative force pulling her to the second-floor room across from the old theater room. Here she felt as if a woman was attacked or even murdered. But due to the fact that the room was occupied, we were told not to enter. Could this have been the spot where the reported rape-murder took place? Later that night while in the top-floor turret room, the film crew was having technical problems while the investigation team was picking up on possible activity. Here the crew found that their monitors were responding to the questions asked by flashing or scrambling "once for yes" and "twice for no." We are not sure who the spirit was trying to make contact with us. However, we do feel there is something lingering in the old Georgetown Castle.

Today, the castle is a private home, but on occasion it is open to the public for the Georgetown Art and Garden Walk. If you happen to catch this event, it is a great opportunity to go inside and maybe see a ghost or two.

See also: The Central Tavern in Pioneer Square; Georgetown Playfield in this section

PLANE CRASHES

Georgetown is directly under the flight path of the Boeing Field, which has paved the way for a tragic history for those who dare live or work around it.

1910: On March 11, the first Seattle airplane took flight from Meadows Race Track just south of Georgetown. William Boeing observed Charles Hamilton's flight from the Duwamish River where his yacht was being built. Just two days later, Mr. Hamilton was injured when he crashed his Curtis Reims Racer aircraft into a pond.

1912: In May, from the same racetrack, many watched what would be Seattle's first aviation death when J. Clifford Turpin crashed into the grandstands during a demonstration, killing one and injuring twenty-one onlookers.

1937: In November two planes collided killing five men, littering the ground with debris and remains over Boeing Field.

1943: In February a Boeing XB-29 top-secret bomber took off from Boeing Field. Shortly after take off, one of the engines caught fire. The pilot turned to land when another fire erupted. By this time, two crew members had bailed out, only to find their parachutes wouldn't open as they fell to their deaths. The bomber, however, slammed into the Frye Packing Plant outside of Boeing Field, killing nine other crew members and nineteen workers.

1949: In January a DC-3 airliner was carrying twenty-seven Yale University students back to Connecticut after the holidays. Although ice on the wings was treated with alcohol, pilot Emmett G. Flood refused to fly the plane. Owner William J. Leland took his place. Families and friends watched as the plane took off and then veered right. The plane crashed into a Boeing hanger and burst into flames, killing eleven students and all three crew members as well as injuring thirteen other passengers.

1949: In July a C-46 airliner from Air Transport Associates lost power in its engine. The pilot then turned the plane around, and it ripped through two power lines before plowing into a house at 961 Harney Street. The plane was carrying twenty-eight military passengers. This tragic event took the lives of seven people—two on the plane and five on the ground.

1951: In August a Boeing B-50 bomber lost power shortly after take off and ended up clipping what was once the Rainer Brewery, causing the plane to cartwheel into the Lester Apartments on Beacon Hill. The four thousand gallons of fuel in the plane caused a huge explosion that took the lives of all six crew members and five residents, leaving eleven injured.

Before their destruction, the Lester Apartments had an intriguing yet seedy history. What had become housing for people with limited or fixed incomes had its beginnings as the world's largest bordello—so proclaimed when construction began in 1910.

At that time, the mayor of Seattle was Hiram Gill, and Gill's chief of police was Charles Wappenstein. Together they ran the city in a less-than-admirable fashion, engaging in many questionable activities. Wappenstein (better known as "Wappy") collected ten dollars a month from each of the more-than-five-hundred working girls in his territory. With the large sums of money collected from the girls, a handshake deal on some property, and a nod from the mayor, construction began on what was to serve as the bordello. The building was designed to hold enough small rooms to house each of the five hundred working girls. Before construction was completed, Gill was removed from office and Wappenstein had been sent to the state penitentiary. Without anyone to see the project to fruition, the structure stood empty. Oddly enough, Gill was reelected in 1914 after he promised to crack down on vice. Sometime later, the five hundred cells were combined to make a number of apartments, mostly used during and after WWII, eventually taking on the name The Lester Apartments.

With sudden and tragic deaths like those that happened in the plane crashes in or near Georgetown, we often find these lost souls can remain behind in their confusion. Some may not even be aware they have passed on. At some of these sites, people have heard the repeating sounds of a crash, smelled burning flesh, and witnessed a flash of light as if something hit the ground. Whether these are intelligent or residual hauntings, they are still hauntings.

COMET LODGE CEMETERY
South Graham and South Twenty-third Streets

What appears to be a lovely little park settled in the middle of a small residential area is actually a cemetery. This resting place started out as Duwamish burial ground known simply as "The Old Burial Grounds." The land was acquired by the Maple Family in the early 1890s and converted into a pioneer cemetery. This became the final resting place for a number of early residents, some of whom were influential in the development of the city. In its prime, this cemetery held more than eight hundred graves. The land quickly filled up, and new burials stopped in the 1930s. The last recorded burial was a child named Jewel Lundin, who passed at three years of age on September 21, 1936.

On November 2, 1987, the City of Seattle began bulldozing the graveyard, ripping up tombstones—what a Day of the Dead surprise for the residents of Comet Lodge! Currently, there are approximately twenty gravestones still standing. So what happened to the remaining seven hundred odd markers? It is believed that as the cemetery fell into disrepair, the city began to sell off parts of the cemetery. After many years of vandalism and neglect, it was easy for the city to deny its presence, claiming that the bodies were moved. Houses were built over parts of the children's section of the cemetery, and now residents claim ghosts of children are living in their homes. In fact, one home appeared on a local TV show addressing their ghost problem that has haunted them for years.

Several families have witnessed odd happenings in their homes. In one house a woman reportedly found the items in her doll collection moved, as if someone had been playing with them. What made this most strange is that she kept all her dolls in a glass case. She claimed to find them lying on the floor or sitting in the chairs throughout her house when she would awake in the morning.

Another family's young son was getting into trouble when he would leave his toys on the floor time and time again. Even though he claimed that he had not touched those toys. The parents didn't believe him and continued to punish him for leaving his toys around the house. It wasn't until their son told them about a boy who would visit him in the night and sit at the edge of his bed that his parents realized something was out of place. The son said the boy was in strange clothes and did not speak but believed he was there to watch over him. Sounds like something from a Hollywood movie!

Others have seen the ghosts roaming through their disrupted resting ground. Lights will appear and then suddenly disappear, and some say bushes and trees will shake even when there is no wind or breeze.

Are the disrupted souls of Seattle's pioneers making it known that they want their old cemetery back? When desecration happens at a burial site, many believe that the spirits will return to take vengeance or find what the ruckus is all about. In any case, hundreds of people have been robbed of their eternal resting spot.

Today, there are efforts to restore the old cemetery to its true beginnings. Many volunteers are helping to find unmarked burial plots and lost tombstones. Slowly, as the years pass, its story of what remains and its history become clearer. Let's hope Comet Lodge Cemetery does return, and maybe in due time the restless spirits will finally find some rest as well.

JULES MAES SALOON
5919 Airport Way S

A two-story brick structure sits on the corner of Airport Way and Nebraska. The interior still contains the original walk-in icebox at the end of the bar, an enormous office safe, and a one-hundred-year-old Brunswick bar that was shipped all the way around Cape Horn. This building dates back to 1898 and was known as "The Brick Store," performing many functions over the years—a grocery and drugstore, tavern, restaurant, meeting hall, hardware store, boarding house, and apartments. When it was known as the "Citizens Club," boxing matches were held on the first floor and pigeon races on the second.

Some say that glasses fly off shelves; things turn up missing; and one employee felt some one standing behind him only to turn and see no one around. Is there something of the afterlife here, or is it the work of another kind of spirits altogether?

GEORGETOWN LIQUOR COMPANY
5501 Airport Way S

This area was built in 1906 and is known as the Bertoldi Block. The Bertoldi family was one of many Italian immigrant families that played an important role in the establishment of the Georgetown commercial and residential areas. Though the establishment is currently known as the Georgetown Liquor Company, it's believed that

GEORGETOWN LIQUOR COMPANY

in its glory days of the early 1900s, the top floor was used as a brothel. Georgetown made its popularity by developing its own red light district. When Prohibition was instituted in the 1930s, many Seattle locals snuck down to this part of town to enjoy its pleasures.

Many have worked in this building throughout the years and have heard what they described as the sounds of lovemaking or the horsing around of a couple coming from the upstairs area, even when there is no one up there at the time. Could these sounds be that of the spirits of lovers who have chosen to remain behind to externally enjoy what might be their own heaven?

Coliman RESTAURANT
6932 Carleton Avenue S

Named after the most active volcano in Mexico, this Mexican restaurant is believed to have a ghost. In the 1940s it was known as Newcastle Restaurant. One night after closing, a man attempted to rob the bartenders. Unannounced to the robber, the authorities were called in and were able to trap him in the northwest corner of the bar. After a short scuffle, the robber was shot and killed by police. It seems that throughout

COLIMAN RESTAURANT

the restaurant's history, guests tend to avoid or even refuse to sit in the particular corner where the man died. Could it be that people unaware of the tragic event can somehow feel his presence still suffering from that night's tragedy?

STEAM PLANT
East off South Warsaw Street

Built in 1909 as one of the first reinforced-concrete structures on the West Coast, this plant supplied power for the railways, the streetcars, and for Georgetown itself. In 1917 it was converted to a coal-fired plant. The Steam Plant discontinued service in 1972 but is surprisingly still fully operational.

Today a museum, people from all over can look into a bit of Seattle's history and the wonders of steam power. There is also something else to consider while visiting this site: many believe it has a ghost who likes to cause disturbances with tools. Pallets loaded with tools have unexplainably begun moving, turning on and off and causing banging noises that can not be traced. Did something bad happen here? Or is this the work of a very devoted worker who still feels the need to come to work?

STEAM PLANT

OLD COUNTRY INN ROADHOUSE
6601 Carleton Avenue S

Now called Carleton Avenue Grocery, this building (built in 1904) has a colorful history of gambling and prostitution. During early 1900s, the Old Country Inn Roadhouse was run by Everett A. Hutchings, also known as "Big Hutch," a big-time thug in the area who was known to steal and to beat and lock men in rooms until debts where paid. Many of these cruel acts happened right here within the building's walls. In 1909 Big Hutch confronted the mayor of Georgetown about stopping the closing of all roadhouses. The

OLD COUNTRY INN ROADHOUSE

meeting ended with Hutchings beating the mayor almost to death. After that, all road-houses where closed in 1910. By 1911 the building opened as a grocery store and has remained so to this day, becoming Seattle's oldest running grocery store.

With its violent history, it's not surprising that there might be a ghost story or two related to this building. Some say you can hear walking by unseen feet and odd sounds and whisperings from voices of the past. There are even stories of the owner's dog barking at a wall that was discovered to be part of a long hallway where many gentlemen would have walked to visit the ladies' dressing rooms. Most believe that these are memories from the past acting themselves out to an audience of the living.

GEORGETOWN PLAYFIELD
750 South Homer Street

This five-plus-acre park stands near what were the grounds of the former King County Almshouse and Hospital. Opened in 1877 by three Catholic nuns known as the Sisters of Charity, the hospital remained open for a year and a half before the sisters moved their work to another location. However, the hospital reopened in 1890 in what was an old farmhouse and remained operational until 1956 when the expanded building was sold and demolished. There are also stories that a small cemetery was situated on the hospital grounds or adjacent to the hospital property.

The King County Almshouse and Hospital was also known as the "Poor Farm" because they took on many unfortunate folks who could not afford the services of a regular hospital. This 125-patient capacity was later expanded to accommodate 225 in 1908. In 1911 tuberculosis had infected the people of Seattle to the point that tents for the contaminated were set up on the hospital grounds, and by 1920 the site was so overrun with the ill that beds had to be placed throughout the corridors. The hospital had so many deaths that they even had their own crematorium to dispose of the bodies. Although now the hospital and cemetery are long gone, perhaps some of its former residents remain in the area.

Folks have enjoyed the park for many years, and since its refurbishment in 2008, you will now find lighted ball fields, a playground, tennis courts, a children's wading pool and, of course, a ghost.

GEORGETOWN PLAYFIELD

Locals and passersby have seen a barefoot woman with long red hair, wearing a long white dress and running through the park late at night. Her transparent image seems to be running from something, but she tends to vanish before anyone can find out who she is or what she is running from. Could she be running to save the life she once had? Perhaps she is playing out a trapped memory of a horrific event that took place here a long time ago. Or could she somehow be tied to the grounds' history?

When the hospital building was demolished, the graves from the adjacent cemetery were also to be moved. Some say not all of the bodies were removed. Those with families to arrange burial were moved to other sites, but some say others were thrown into the Duwamish River. And what if some of the bodies were missed? What if some remain? Perhaps the barefooted ghost has something to do with spirits who are not at rest. If ever you visit the park and see this lovely apparition, see if you can get her to speak with you before she vanishes.

See also: The Georgetown Castle in this section

MUSEUM OF FLIGHT
9404 East Marginal Way S

Established in 1965, this nonprofit museum is the largest private air and space museum in the world with more then eighty aircraft lining the grounds and suspended above. Here you will find the first presidential jet, VC-137B SAM 970, which served from 1959 to 1996; the only Concorde west of the Appalachians; a Caproni Ca.20, the world's first fighter plane, from World War I; one of only two remaining flyable Douglas DC-2s; the only surviving Boeing 80A, flown by Bob Reeve in Alaska; and many more to tease your taste buds for flight history.

Many of these aircraft served in the wars and survived fatalities—some were even restored from plane wreckage. So would it be a surprise that many spirits have been attached to these empty shells? Guests and museum staff believe this to be true, as they constantly see the apparition of a pilot in a brown leather jack sitting in the cockpit of one of the suspended planes. His spirit has also been seen wandering among the other airplanes, looking ever so curiously at them. Could he be interested in how aviation had changed through the years? Some security guards have heard foots steps echoing through the empty building late at night when no one else is around, and at times they get a whiff of cigar smoke followed by a short breeze, as if the ghost walked on by.

Who is this mystery pilot? Could he be someone who died in one of the museum's planes? Or is he just a man who loved flying so much he is not ready to let go of that freedom?

MUSEUM OF FLIGHT

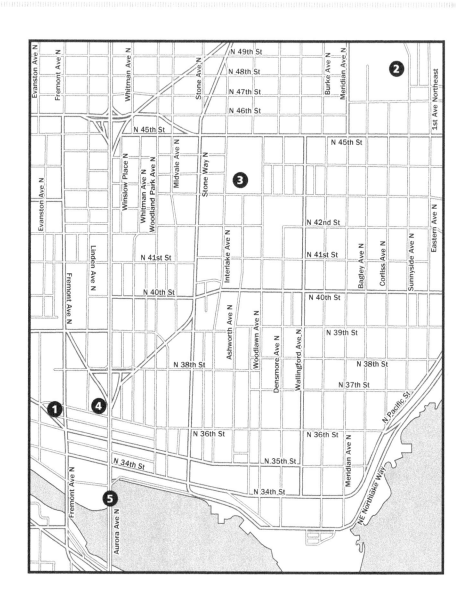

10. FREMONT

Established in the 1880s as a lumber-mill town, it was annexed to Seattle in 1891. It was named after Fremont, Nebraska, the hometown of two of its founders, and was also known as the "Center of the Universe." After the 1989 fall of the Communist government, the controversial statue of Lenin was salvaged from Slovakia and given a new home here, by a local art lover who was teaching in the area at the time. This area is also home to the famed Fremont Troll, a piece of public art, under the Aurora Bridge. Here you will also find helpful advice on some of the local street signs, such as "Set your watch ahead five minutes," "Set your watch back five minutes," and "Throw your watch away." Other landmarks include an old rocket fuselage and the outdoor sculpture *Waiting for the Interurban*.

Fremont is also home to the historic B.F. Day School, which was founded in 1891 after Seattle annexed the Fremont neighborhood, making it the longest continually operating school in the Seattle school district

In the summer you might want to see the nude cyclists at the Summer Solstice Parade and Pageant. In the fall, the annual Trolloween event is always fun.

MAP MARKERS

1. Deluxe Junk
2. The Good Shepherd Center
3. Hamilton Middle School
4. The Fremont Troll
5. Aurora Bridge

DELUXE JUNK
3518 Fremont Place N

This retro shop sits under the Masonic Temple built in 1909. The space was first a funeral home run by Fisher & Milton in 1928 and then bought by Hoffner & Putnam in 1946. They closed down the funeral parlor in the late 1970s.

In 1978 Deluxe Junk settled in to these quarters, turning the space into the shop you see today. If you do get the chance to venture to this location, you'll clearly see the alcoves where coffins were laid out for mourners to select their loved ones' caskets. Throughout the lower half of the building you can see other signs of its old occupation, such as the coffin-loading area, where the dead would be brought in and the viewing rooms for those in mourning paying their last respects. Maybe its funereal history has to do with what employees and the owners have felt here—more specifically, a presence in the backroom. They hear strange noises, and things have been known to fall off selves for unknown reasons. Some say have they have seen, out of the corners of their eyes, ghostly figures moving, and when they turn to look more closely, the ghostly figures vanish.

DELUXE JUNK

THE GOOD SHEPHERD CENTER

4649 Sunnyside Avenue N

In 1890 five Roman Catholic Sisters of Our Lady of the Good Shepherd, from St. Paul, Minnesota, arrived by train to the streets of Seattle. Their goal was to open and operate a home for wayward girls. The Sisters had the good fortune to eventually settle in a building on Sunnyside Avenue, designed and constructed by the architectural firm of Breitung and Buchinger (principal architects: Carl Alfred Breitung and Theobald Buchinger) in 1906. They named their home for wayward girls The Home of the Good Shepherd.

The Sisters maintained a strict environment for all who stayed in The Home of the Good Shepherd. The unfortunate girls under the nuns' care were referred to as Keepsakes for Heaven or Fallen Girls. The young ladies who lived in the home had their sleeping quarters assigned to them according to their behavioral status: good girls lived in the north wing; troublesome girls lived in the south wing.

THE GOOD SHEPHERD CENTER

In 1967 an intense fire damaged the fifth floor of the south wing. No one was seriously harmed in the fire, but negative energy remained. Six years later, in June of 1973, the home was forced to close its doors forever due to the falling numbers of girls seeking assistance. In 1975 the city of Seattle acquired the property to use as a community center, and in 1984 the property received landmark status and recognition on The National Register of Historic Places.

Known to locals as both The Sunnyside Center and The Good Shepherd Center, the building houses a number of schools and nonprofit organizations. Among the occupants are the Neo Art School, the Wallingford Senior Center, and a number of artists' studios.

Today, those who work in the building and visitors alike have had strange experiences. Some say they can still hear the voices of the young girls echoing from down the halls. Others have claimed to see apparitions of the girls, dancing or sitting as if in a classroom.

Is it possible that some of the building's past continues to play out memories from its history? What seems to stand out most is the sighting of a nun, who doesn't seem to be a memory but more of an active ghost who still looks after the building. She has been spotted wandering the halls, sitting in the garden, and even working in the old classrooms. Her presence is often felt, but it is most often when something mischievous is happening. This nun seems to have no problem letting anyone know that she will not tolerate any misbehavior in her school!

HAMILTON MIDDLE SCHOOL
4400 Interlake Avenue N

This 1940s building is suspected of having ghosts. Many report hearing footsteps while alone on the second floor. The doors are known to inexplicably open and close, and doorknobs will shake if locked. Story has it that a plumber died of a heart attack in the second-floor girls' bathroom, but he was not discovered until after his shift. Many claim to see a face in the mirrors; in fact, the mirrors in that bathroom are reported to break at least three times a year. Could this be the work of an unsettled spirit? Of course, it could be the wind, but its more fun to think it's the work of the Hamilton Middle School Ghost!

HAMILTON MIDDLE SCHOOL

THE FREMONT TROLL

North Thirty-sixth Street (under Aurora Bridge)

Lurking under the Aurora Bridge is the eighteen-foot concrete sculpture of a troll created in 1990. This monster of a beast is crushing an actual Volkswagen Beetle in its left hand. The troll was sculpted by four Seattle-area artists (Steve Badanes, Will Martin, Donna Walter, and Ross Whitehead) for the Fremont Arts Council when they were approached about doing something imaginative with the space under the Aurora Bridge. The sculpture is made from rebar steel, wire, and about two tons of messy ferroconcrete. With lots of hard work, the troll sculpture took about seven weeks to complete.

Rumor has it that prior to the sculpture's installation, many old-time residents told of sightings of a real troll roaming about the neighborhood. The community also pays tribute to the troll every October 31 with the "Trolloween" party. This celebration begins under the bridge and participants then wander to other spooky sites and events in Fremont.

THE FREMONT TROLL

AURORA BRIDGE
Highway 99 (between Fremont and Queen Anne neighborhoods)

Built in 1932 as the George Washington Memorial Bridge, the Aurora Bridge is more commonly known as Suicide Bridge. The bridge received this name for the more than 230 people who have jumped to their deaths from its surface. Standing 167 feet above water, it also holds the second-highest recorded number of suicides in the United States, trailing behind the Golden Gate Bridge. The first suicide occurred in January 1932, when a shoe salesman dropped from the bridge before it was completed. When it comes to suicide, many believe that these troubled souls remain earthbound. Therefore, claims of lingering apparitions appearing to reenact their final moments are not too surprising. There is a report of a troubled man jumping from the bridge while carrying his beloved dog. There have been stories of a man and his dog wandering around the bridge just staring at passersby. But when they turn back to see if the man is still looking, he is completely gone!

In November of 1998 the Seattle metro bus system faced its worst accident in its twenty-five year history. While crossing the bridge southbound, a passenger on the bus shot and killed the driver for unknown reasons and then turned the .38 automatic

Haunting Fact

The one thing most commonly remembered about a deceased loved one is their scent. Perhaps what remains is a favorite perfume or cologne or simply their normal smell. Many grieving individuals report smelling certain scents of the lost loved one when there's nothing in the room to cause the scent. Many believe that spirits can carry a smell with them and that the living can detect these smells. Maybe the spirits want to remind their loved ones that they are still around and watching them

pistol on himself. The driver lost control, veering across two lanes of traffic. The bus plunged off the bridge's eastern side, dropping fifty feet onto the roof of an apartment building near where the Fremont Troll dwells. One passenger was killed while thirty-two other passengers survived with injuries. Whether something remains of this horrific event, let's pray their spirits are not continuing to relive that terrible day.

AURORA BRIDGE

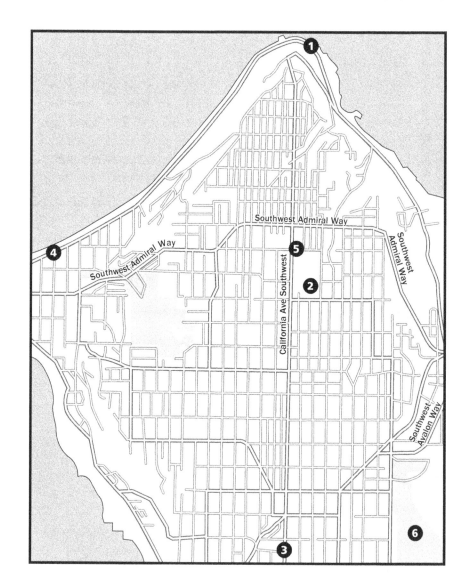

11. WEST SEATTLE

West Seattle is where the first white settlers, the Denny party, began laying ground for the city at Alki Point. Naming their new town, New York Alki. But the settlers could not survive the open weather conditions, being surrounded by the waters. So after the harsh winter they packed up and crossed the bay to begin again. As this location is where settlers first touched ground, it can be argued that West Seattle is the city's oldest neighborhood. Here you will find the marker where the first settlement was, and on Alki Beach you will find a mini Statue of Liberty to remind Seattle citizens of a name they almost had. The major highlights of this area are the Gatewood area, Seattle's highest point, and the breathtaking views of the Olympic Mountains.

MAP MARKERS

1. Luna Park
2. West Seattle High School
3. Rite-Aid

4. Homestead Restaurant
5. Hiawatha Playfield
6. Camp Long

LUNA PARK

Alki Beach Park (located at the tip)

Opened in 1907, Luna Park was an amusement park designed by Charles I. D. Looff, who was known for carving and setting up the first carousel in Coney Island, New York. His carousel was designed for Coney Island's Luna Park, giving Seattle's Luna Park the nickname the "Coney Island of the West."

Seattle's Luna Park was built not far from where the original settlers landed in 1851 in West Seattle. In the beginning, West Seattle was a separate town from Seattle, but reachable by a quick ferry ride across the bay. Like Coney Island's Luna Park, Seattle's park was built out over the water. Rides, attractions, and all kinds of entertainment filled the park.

All of the buildings and attractions were outlined with light bulbs, giving the park great visibility from distances, including from downtown Seattle. People came from all over the state to experience the attractions of Luna Park. Who could resist the wonders of the Canals of Venice, the Cave of Mystery, and the Figure 8 Roller Coaster! Guests could enjoy the rides, eat, play games, listen to music, and swim in the freshwater and saltwater pools of the natatorium. Long after Luna Park's closure, the natatorium remained open as Luna Pool.

LUNA PARK

One of the most popular attractions was Looff's Zeum Carousel. Charles I.D. Looff built Luna Park's Zeum Carousel in Rhode Island. The design was similar to the one he made for Luna Park, Coney Island. Originally, the carousel was intended for the city of San Francisco, but due to the fire and the earthquake, the carousel landed in Seattle's Luna Park in time for its opening in 1907.

Luna Park had a fire in 1911, with most attractions suffering damage. Only the carousel escaped unscathed. After Luna Park closed in 1913, the carousel was dismantled and shipped to its original destination, San Francisco. Upon arrival in California, the carousel was restored and operated at Playland-at-the-Beach until the park closed in 1972.

The carousel was once again dismantled and boxed. Rather than shipping the carousel to a new home, the pieces remained in boxes and were sent to a storage facility in Roswell, New Mexico. In 1983, California leased the carousel, which found a temporary home in Long Beach, until moved finally to its current home, Yerba Buena Gardens, in . . . San Francisco!

Although there were many family pleasures to be found at Luna Park, the community was not so happy that the park maintained what it called "the longest and best-stocked bar" in the area. Seattle's mayor promised to maintain strict morality in Seattle, but Luna Park was in West Seattle. Two days after Luna Park opened, the more liberal town of West Seattle was annexed by Seattle. This act did little to threaten the pleasures of the bar, but the townspeople were ever watchful.

On January 31, 1911, a newspaper ran an article claiming that girls of fourteen were seen carousing with the drunkards of Luna Park, drinking beer and smoking cigarettes. Finding itself connected with political and moral scandals, it seemed the days of the park were numbered. In fact, a fire in 1911 did quite some damage to the park's attractions. The fire did not put an end to Luna Park, but in 1913 the park closed its gates permanently. Rides were dismantled. Buildings were torn down. All that survived was the swimming area, the natatorium, then called Luna Pool. In 1931 the pier was set ablaze by an arsonist's match on April 14. Although no one was hurt in the fire, the damage was so great that the pier was condemned in 1933.

Today, when many downtown residents and tourists happen to look across the bay to where Luna Park once stood they sometimes see, to their surprise, a fire. This blaze has been reported to the fire department, but it is always a false alarm. People on the Alki beaches see no fire, but some locals on the beaches have reported the smell of something burning. The odd thing is, all these reports are made only around April 14.

WEST SEATTLE HIGH SCHOOL

3000 California Avenue S

The building opened in 1902 as West Seattle School and was renamed West Seattle High School in 1917. Stories say that a student named Rose Higginbotham may have hung herself here in 1924, but no records prove this. Many students claim to have seen her roaming the school. There are also claims of a photo featuring her peering out the window. Her spirit has also been seen wandering in the nearby park. There's no conclusive evidence who this ghostly woman is or if it is the spirit of Rose, but the claims of a young woman's ghost dressed in 1920s-era clothing seem to and will continue to haunt the minds of the students at West Seattle High School .

See also: Hiawatha Playfield in this section

WEST SEATTLE HIGH SCHOOL

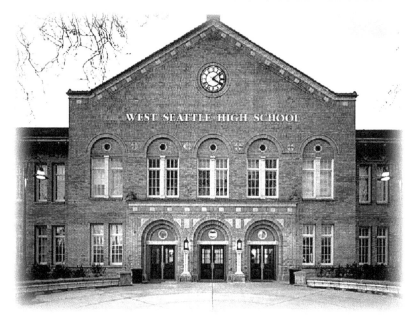

RITE-AID

5217 California Avenue SW

It seems to be your run-of-the-mill Rid-Aid—but with a supernatural twist. Strange things have happened to employees—sink taps turning water on full blast, lights turning off, false alarms constantly going off, and banging sounds heard from unknown sources. No one knows for sure who or what is haunting this site. Some say the building was constructed over an old coal mine where many men had died in cave-ins. Employees absolutely do not like being alone here.

RITE-AID

HOMESTEAD RESTAURANT

2717 Sixty-first Avenue SW

As of 2009 all that remains of this last surviving log structure on Alki Point is a burned out shell. How it got to this point is a very interesting question. The building was erected in 1904 by the Bernard Family who lived there until 1907. Once known as the Fir Lodge, it became the Alki Homestead Restaurant in 1950.

Throughout the years there have been weird things happening at Homestead. Many employees talked about strange noises of people running or walking upstairs, but when investigated, there would be no one up there. Glasses had been known to fly

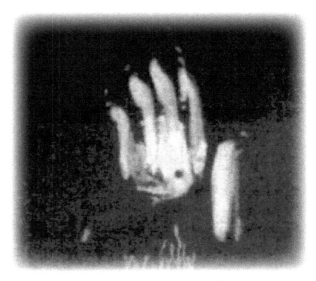

HAND PRINT FOUND ON BURNT WALL AT
HOMESTEAD RESTAURANT

off tables and dishes have fallen from shelves. At one point, a commercial refrigerator door came off its hinges and flew across the room smashing into a bar of glasses. The owner would receive dead phone calls from the restaurant throughout the night, when no one was there to call. The restaurant started to have small electrical fires and false fire alarms in the middle of the night. The owner concerned of the ghosts called upon a Chinese psychic for answers. Her reply was the spirits were not at rest nor were they happy, and she warned him of a great fire.

With the warnings and the increase in activity, the owner was in search of answers and ways to appease the spirits within his restaurant. Employees had stated that the odd noises were getting louder as the energies become more destructive. More and more dishes would fall off tables and shelves or were found broken. The voiceless phone calls from the restaurant continued and the smells of things burning were in the air, but no sign of any fires.

In January of 2009 the inside burned down early one Friday morning, causing more then $400,000 in damages. But this was not the last of the spirits that haunted within it walls. When the building was inspected the following day, the contractor felt something odd about the place. On further inspection, hand prints began to show up all over the place within the charcoal-and-smoke-covered walls. When it was reported that no one had been in the building after the fire, the contractor left, but only after taking pictures of the hand prints and scratches.

Activity like this is extremely rare, which interested the AGHOST team when contacted by employees after the last fire. But due to liabilities of an unsafe environment, an investigation could not be set up at the time. However, it is rumored that the restaurant will reopen and the team hopes to look into its aggressive activity for any future owner. But the question is: could the spirits be at rest now? Or is there a bigger message they'd like to pass on before they move on?

HIAWATHA PLAYFIELD
2700 California Avenue SW

An Olmstead Legacy Park opened in 1911, Hiawatha Playfield was named in honor of the hero of Longfellow's poem "The Song of Hiawatha." The sixteenth-century Mohawk chieftain, who was famed for his miraculous powers, brought about the Five National Confederation of Indians known as the League of Iroquois, and roamed through the forests of northern Michigan. In Hiawatha Playfield, at sunset and sunrise, during

HIAWATHA PLAYFIELD

periods of heavy fog, or on deeply overcast days, the apparition of Rose Higginbotham, a student that may have hung herself at West Seattle High School, has been seen. Some also claimed to have seen ghostly animals wandering the park grounds.

See also: West Seattle High School in this section

CAMP LONG
5200 Thirty-fifth Avenue SW

With sixty-eight acres of wilderness, Camp Long is a true getaway for those who like to hike, rock climb, and camp in rustic cabins. Once reserved for private children's clubs, Camp Long opened to the public in 1984. In 1937, during the Great Depression, a group of individuals pitched in to invest in the youth. The creators of the park used whatever materials were available. Lumber for the cabins came from abandoned structures. The camp's lodge used old stone paving blocks from a repaved street. Shrubs and trees came from a bankrupt nursery. Finally, in 1941 the Camp Long opened.

With all those materials from times of hardship, is it possible some spirits have attached themselves to the camp? Many have felt that some of the cabins have lodged more than the living. There have also been reports of strange noises and things being moved around with no explanation.

CAMP LONG

Haunting Fact

Children seem to have an easier time than adults interacting with ghosts. In many cases, the ghost may be perceived as an imaginary friend. Researchers have found that the children will report information only known to a deceased family member or a previous resident of the property. Children grow up with an open mind and seem to have the ability to perceive spirits, but when loved ones reassure frightened children that ghosts do *not* exist, these perceptions begin to change. Telling children that ghosts are not real is a step in conditioning a child's beliefs and developing a more closed idea of the spirit world.

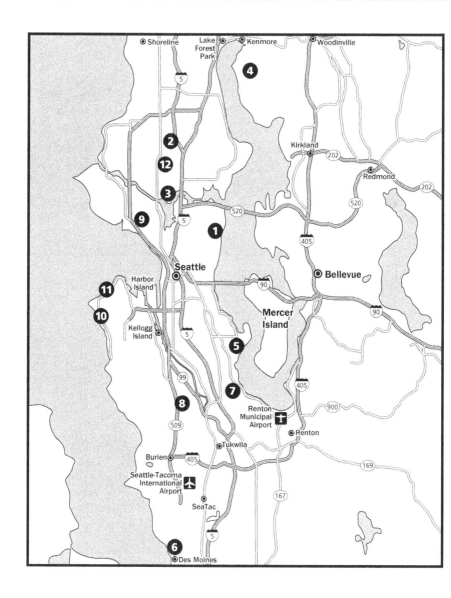

12. SEATTLE PARKS

Seattle has always been known as "The Evergreen State" because of its lush evergreen trees. It features some of the most beautiful parks on the West Coast, with Seattle's Parks and Recreation tending to literally hundreds of parks. But along with the great beauty of these parks come ghostly presences as well. Denny Park, Seattle's oldest park, holds many secrets above and below ground. But how many of Seattle's other parks hold similar secrets?

MAP MARKERS

1. Kurt Cobain's Bench
2. Green Lake
3. Gas Works Park
4. St. Edwards State Park
5. Martha Washington School and Park
6. Des Moines Marina Park
7. Kubota Garden
8. Glen Acres Golf and Country Club
9. Kinnear Park
10. Me-Kwa-Mooks Park
11. Schmitz Park
12. Woodland Park

KURT COBAIN'S BENCH

171 Lake Washington Boulevard E

Just across the street from Viretta Park sits a house that once belonged to legendary grunge rocker Kurt Cobain of Nirvana. On April 8, 1994 Kurt Cobain decided to take his own life with the assistance of a shotgun. An employee discovered his body in the spare room above the garage. Some say his death may have been murder and not suicide.

It is believed that before his death Kurt spent most of his remaining days sitting on a bench just outside his house. Maybe that's where he planned his last moments. Whether or not it's true, people say that they can feel his presence near the bench. Others say they have seen him just sitting there, reliving his last few hours. Some have even reported feeling him breathe on them or touch them. In fact, there have

KURT COBAIN'S BENCH

been reports of his face appearing in the window of his former home, and the new owners say that during thunderstorms, they can hear whispers from the former rock star himself. If you visit this site, you'll find a bench filled with flowers and cards and writings from fans who miss his inspirational talent.

The city parks department must replace the boards on the bench every so often due to the graffiti left by fans. One man believes he has obtained the original boards that Kurt himself sat on just before that tragic event. After collecting these boards and placing them on his property, the man immediately began encountering strange things. He felt a chilling breeze shoot right past him, as if someone had run by him. He's heard odd noises and felt a presence, and he believes that Kurt's spirit might be attached to these boards.

Many believe that the spirit of one who commits suicide remains earthbound, due to its troubled state of mind at the time of death. So perhaps Kurt's ghost lingers as one of those hurting souls who may have regret.

GREEN LAKE
5701 East Green Lake Way

This 323-acre park, created in 1903, surrounds the waters of Green Lake itself. Impressed with its beauty, some would never guess what a horrific event took place on its shores.

A pair of women's shoes was found lying next to Green Lake on Thursday morning, June 17, 1926. A carpenter was on his way to work when he stumbled upon the shoes. Looking for their owner, he stumbled a few feet further and found the body of twenty-two-year-old Sylvia Gaines.

When the authorities searched the murder scene, they deduced that Sylvia had been murdered in one location, and her body was then dragged several yards to where she was found. Her clothes were torn, and her body was arranged in a way that suggested rape. She had been strangled and struck with a weapon. A bloody rock was found in the nearby vicinity.

The story of Sylvia caught Seattle's attention, and her mysterious death remained front-page news for months. Sylvia was in Seattle to establish a relationship with her estranged father, whom she had not seen since she was five years old. She was born in Massachusetts, and her father moved to Washington State after her parents divorced.

GREEN LAKE

After graduating from Smith College, Sylvia journeyed west to meet and get to know her father. Exactly what kind of relationship this father and daughter developed was a large part of the murder case!

No one wanted to believe that a father would kill his daughter. The King County prosecutor, Ewing Colvin, was among those who refused to believe such a horrible thing might be true. But there was too much evidence pointing towards a questionable relationship between Sylvia and her father, Wallace C. Bob Gaines.

When Sylvia arrived in Seattle, she stayed with Gaines and his wife, who lived in a one-bedroom house. While Gaines and his wife shared the bedroom, Sylvia slept on the couch. Rumor had it that Mrs. Gaines had caught Mr. Gaines and daughter in compromising positions and that the three often fought. It was proposed that perhaps Gaines and his daughter were sharing the bed, while Mrs. Gaines slept on the couch.

Whatever happened behind closed doors, the Gaines family also aired their dirty laundry in public. Both Mr. and Mrs. Gaines were often seen fighting publicly with Sylvia. And during the trial, several witnesses testified to catching Mr. Gaines and Sylvia in questionable acts, including a police officer who had caught Gaines and his daughter parked in a car late at night . . . talking. The most damaging evidence in the case came from Gaines' drinking buddy, Louis Stern, who testified that Gaines visited him while drunk and all but confessed to murdering Sylvia.

It was suggested that Sylvia left the Gaines home on the evening of June 16 to get away from her father, and he killed her to prevent her from leaving or revealing the truth of their relationship. Gaines was found guilty and sentenced to death. He was hanged for the murder of Sylvia Gaines on August 31, 1928.

Shortly after the murder, the community came to the park and planted cottonwood trees, which were removed in 1999 and replaced with Populus x robusta on the northern part, and the location was named Gaines Point in honor of her. Today, visitors see the transparent figure of a young woman walking on the trails here. Many have heard her sobbing late into the night. Ghost investigators have even captured a possible recording of her trying to answer their questions. Is she trying to pass on a message? Is this why she is still seen today strolling through the dimly lit park at night? Is there something still left undone?

GAS WORKS PARK
2101 North Northlake Way

This is a nineteen-acre park on the site of the former Seattle Gas Light Company, which operated from 1906 to 1956, and was opened as a city park 1975. It has been called the strangest park in Seattle (and possibly the world). One thing that might add to its strangeness is the fact that all of the trees in Gas Works Park are potted because nothing will take root deeper than three feet. It is believed that the park was built on a Native American burial ground.

GAS WORKS PARK

Many visitors have reported seeing Native Americans in traditional clothes walking in the park at dusk. There are also stories of a small boy who continually runs around the old ruins. He can be seen running around the site, and when he is out of sight and expected to show up on the other side, he is never seen again. Is it possible a young boy might have died here?

ST. EDWARDS STATE PARK
14445 Juanita Drive NE

St. Edwards State Park was once the 316-acre property of a Catholic seminary with three thousand feet of shoreline on Lake Washington. In the late 1920s the land was donated by Bishop O'Dea to the Diocese of Seattle for use by the Sulpician order of Catholic priests. In 1931 Saint Edward's Seminary was built and then expanded to a school for theology and collegiate students in 1958. Due to declining enrollment, the diocese sold everything to the state of Washington for use as a state park in 1977. By 1978, the property became what it is today.

For years, people have felt this place is haunted. There have been reports of children seen and heard playing around the playground in the middle of the night,

ST. EDWARDS STATE PARK

when clearly there is no one there. Inside the building, folks have seen things move, smelled strange odors, and experienced odd things happening in the basement areas. There was a young man who died in the 1980s after falling from a third floor window. Could he be lingering on the property?

MARTHA WASHINGTON SCHOOL AND PARK
6612 Fifty-seventh Avenue S

Don't go looking for the Martha Washington School for Girls. The buildings no longer exist. After rumors and complaints of unusual activity on the grounds and in the vacant buildings, Seattle's City Council voted to demolish the structures in 1989. Today, those who venture to this site will find Martha Washington Park on the grounds of the former school.

Before it was fitted as a public park, this property changed hands many times and belonged to a number of Seattle's earliest schoolteachers. Schoolteacher David Graham traded this property to his brother Walter (an employee of Yesler's Mill),

MARTHA WASHINGTON SCHOOL AND PARK

who planted an orchard on the land. When poison oak made the land undesirable, Graham sold the property to Asa Mercer, also a teacher, but mostly famous for his "Mercer Girls." To accommodate the overabundant collection of single males in the Seattle area, Mercer traveled to the San Francisco area, collected single women, and transported them back to Seattle. While stranded in San Francisco with a group of girls, Mercer borrowed a large sum from John Wilson. Mercer, in turn, used the property to pay back his debt to Wilson.

All of these events took place before 1889 when Wilson sold the property to Juvenile Court Judge Everett T. Smith. Five acres of land complete with a large house, a nursery, a boathouse, and a caretaker's cottage made up the property Smith referred to as "Morningside." In 1919, Smith sold "Morningside" to the Seattle School District, which developed the property as the Girls' Parental School.

Through the 1920s and 1930s, the school district added to the property and built up the school. Additional buildings were constructed, including a combination classroom-and-dormitory building and a gymnasium. After a number of renovations, in 1931 the school district renamed the school The Martha Washington School for our nation's original first lady. The city regulated the school until the state of Washington assumed control in 1957. The school remained state owned and operated until 1965 when the state decided to close the residential school.

The property continued to operate as a series of alternative educational institutions, including a Montessori school, for the next few years, but the property was eventually sold back to the City of Seattle in 1972. A year later, the city handed over operations of the property to the Parks Department.

Rumors of suicide, murder, and other violent acts always encircled the school. Those who lived in the area continually asked that the school be relocated. When the building was abandoned in the early 1970s, things only became worse for the neighborhood. New rumors that a satanic cult was holding rituals, including animal sacrifice, in the building finally motivated Seattle's City Council to tear down the buildings, clear out the property, and make Martha Washington School for Girls into Martha Washington Park.

Although no structures continue to stand, all of the trees remain. Reports of strange occurrences on this property continue to surface, particularly involving the trees. Some say that the energy from the students remains on the grounds through the trees that were planted by the students! Others talk of a very dark force that lurks about at night chasing visitors away.

DES MOINES MARINA PARK

22030 Cliff Avenue S

What is to some a great place to jog, picnic, and play is to others a great place to hunt ghosts. The park is the location where the city of Des Moines was founded and features a playground and housing facilities for other events. But on January 8, there's on event you don't want to miss.

There is a strong belief that a little girl named Diana returns every year to the place where she may have died. Her spirit has been seen walking along the beach and swinging on the swings. Many have witnessed a single swing moving on its own while the others remain perfectly still. During AGHOST investigations, there have also been odd EMF readings on the same swing, where there should be none. Some feel there may be other ghostly children hanging around the park. At one time there was a children's home just up the hill, and they would bring the children down to play. Could Diana have been one of those kids?

Others have felt an older man whom they believed worked as a caretaker on the grounds, but his spirit is not a very pleasant one. Some have felt as if they were pushed by him, and he has been known to throw rocks at people passing by. We are not sure who is haunting this park. However, it's best not wander here after dusk.

DES MOINES MARINA PARK

KUBOTA GARDEN

KUBOTA GARDEN
9817 Fifty-fifth Avenue S

Kubota Garden was established in 1927 by a Japanese emigrant, Fujitaro Kubota, who dreamed of a garden that reflected his heritage. With a collection of rare Asian plants, this place gives you the feeling that you are in another country. But that's not the only feeling you get when you venture across the Heart Bridge (constructed in the 1930s, it is one of the oldest structures in the park). Many say they feel a rush of souls pass through them whenever they cross from west to east.

During World War II, the Japanese emigrants were rounded up and placed in internment camps, leaving the gardens abandoned until 1942, when the Kubota family came back and rebuilt it. Today, is what some folks feel on the bridge the lost souls of those rushed to the camps?

GLEN ACRES GOLF COURSE AND COUNTRY CLUB
1000 South 112th Street

This country club was established by Seattle's Jewish community in 1924. It was built as a nine-hole, eighteen-tee golf course. It is also believed to be haunted, as it was believed to have been built on the site of ancient Native American burial grounds (or the grounds had sacred value to them). Between 1956 and 1976, a sizable number of police tried to investigate sightings of a naked man running around the golf course. Once witnessed by the officers themselves as they gave chase, the naked male vanished without a trace just as they cornered him. If this is a sacred site for Native Americans, perhaps that explains the phantom of the naked man, since some witnesses have seen a naked man doing what appears to be a ritual dance in the area of Tenth Avenue S and South 110th Street.

GLEN ACRES GOLF COURSE

KINNEAR PARK
899 West Olympic Place

This area is named after George Kinnear, who is famous for developing the first wagon road from Seattle through the Snoqualmie Pass. Kinnear owned many properties in and around the Seattle area and eventually sold fourteen acres to Seattle to help build a park. These fourteen acres went for one dollar!

Today, some folks claim to hear what sounds like a crying baby. These reports happen mostly at night, but a few have reported the same in the daytime. Could this be the final resting spot for a lost child? Or did something worse happen here?

KINNEAR PARK

ME -KWA-MOOKS PARK
4452 Beach Drive SW

This fifteen-acre, woodsy park on the waterfront is a great place to relax if you are in the West Seattle area. But many locals believe that this park holds the remains of Native Americans. Some locals will point out a grassy area that runs along Beach Drive SW as Native burial grounds, and one elderly woman has no trouble yelling from her

ME-KWA-MOOKS PARK

house across the street for visitors to step off their graves. Considering that the local Natives did bury their dead along the waterfronts, this claim is possibly true. This also could explain why many late-night visitors have seen Native Americans walking along the beaches. Some have even been seen walking in the park as well. Could the locals be right? Could there be a cemetery on these grounds?

SCHMITZ PARK
5501 Southwest Admiral Way

Ferdinand Schmitz, a German immigrant of Seattle pioneer days, watched as Seattle logged all of its natural beauty away with more and more of the forests disappearing. In 1908 Schmitz donated this park to the city as a natural preserve.

A local legend says a man, known as the Rainbow Man, haunts these woods. Supposedly, he emits a rainbow light that attracts children—and if they get too close, they will disappear forever. You might see his victims' small footprints in various rainbow colors or colorful child-like hand prints on the trees. Some even say you can hear the sounds of those lost souls crying. Maybe parents told their children these stories to keep them from going too far into the woods. Or is there some truth behind the legend of Rainbow Man?

WOODLAND PARK
Aurora Avenue N and North Fifty-ninth Street

This ninety-acre park, with Aurora Avenue N (State Route 99) dividing the park in half, actually appears to be two parks. The area that lies to the west of Aurora Avenue N includes a zoo and a rose garden. The area to the east is a more casual environment with jogging trails, athletic fields, and picnic areas. The two areas are connected by bridges over the highway.

In 1889, Guy C. Phinney, a real estate developer, procured this land to be his personal estate. Phinney was also the namesake for the nearby Phinney Ridge neighborhood. When developing the land, he wanted the estate to have a menagerie or small zoo within its boundaries, hence the idea for the Woodland Park Zoo.

Phinney died in 1893, and some time between 1899 and 1900, Seattle's City Council voted to purchase the land from the Phinney estate. In 1902 they hired a Boston firm, Olmsted Brothers, to design the city's park system including Woodland Park. Much time and money was invested in procuring this ground, much to the chagrin of many citizens who felt the park was too far away from town. Although Phinney had established one trolley line and the city another, it took the city a few years to warm up to the benefits of Woodland Park.

Today, lots of people enjoy the zoo, the trails, and the lawn bowling. Woodland Park has become a great place to relax and enjoy its many offerings. However, Woodland Park is not without its haunts.

Near the perimeter of the park, there is a statue of Carlos Torres. Many claim to feel as if the statue is watching them. Others claim that the statue holds a connection with the ghost of Torres. A champion of the poor, Torres's ghost reportedly patrols the area near his statue and attempts to help homeless people. There are also reports of someone crying "Viva la Revolution" in the wee hours of the morning, particularly on holidays.

WOODLAND PARK

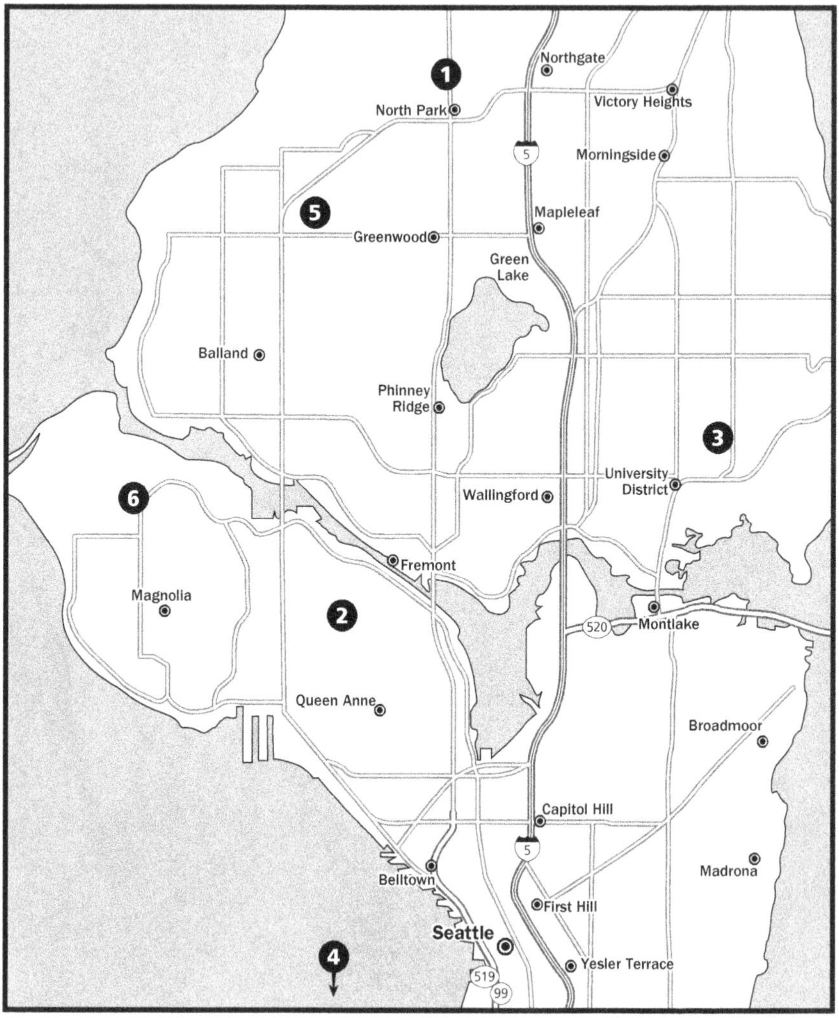

Northgate
①
Victory Heights
North Park
5
Morningside
Mapleleaf
⑤
Greenwood
Green
Lake
Balland
Phinney
Ridge
③
University
District
Wallingford
⑥
Fremont
Magnolia
②
520 Montlake
Queen Anne
Broadmoor
Capitol Hill
5
Belltown
Madrona
First Hill
Seattle
④
Yesler Terrace
519
99

13. SEATTLE CEMETERIES

Seattle has had lots of cemeteries since the settlers came here in 1851. Comet Lodge, Grand Army of the Republic (G.A.R.), and the crown jewel of Seattle's cemeteries, Lake View Cemetery, are covered in other chapters of this book. But there are interesting stories of reports of hauntings in other Seattle cemeteries.

MAP MARKERS

1. Evergreen-Washelli
2. Mount Pleasant
3. Calvary

4. Forest Lawn
5. Crown Hill
6. Fort Lawton

EVERGREEN -WASHELLI

11111 Aurora Avenue N

This cemetery began as Oak Lake Cemetery in the early 1880s. A number of pioneers are buried here with burial sites dating back as early as 1884. However, there was some disturbance to the burial ground in the late 1880s. By 1890 the cemetery was well established, but graves were moved three and even four times to accommodate Seattle's ordinance creating a park out of the cemetery.

The name Washelli is the Makah Indian word for "west wind." Oak Lake was given the name Washelli when the Denny family sold it in 1913. The American Necropolis Corporation bought the cemetery for $ 27,500. In 1922 the cemetery combined with Evergreen Cemetery Company of Seattle, giving the area its current name Evergreen-Washelli Cemetery.

In addition to the combination of two cemeteries to make a larger cemetery, there are a number of sections within the whole that are set aside for different groups.

EVERGREEN-WASHELLI

There are sections devoted to various religious groups, and other sections are set aside for vrious organizations and ethnic groups. Of special note are the sections of the cemetery set aside for veterans and civic service workers, such as firefighters and police. Among those buried in Evergreen-Washelli are a number of the Denny Party members and Marion Anthony Zioncheck, an ostentatious Seattle Democratic Congressman who committed suicide.

Those who have walked in this cemetery at dusk, or even walked nearby at night, often report strange things. Some talk about a ghost dog wandering the grounds that barks if anyone gets too close. Near the mausoleum, many visitors hear walking when no one else is around. This had been heard so often that ghost fanatics were constantly sneaking in to witness this phenomena, and the cemetery had to keep the doors locked to all except those visiting the graves of their loved ones buried there.

See also: Arctic Club in Pioneer Square

MOUNT PLEASANT
700 West Raye Street

The cemetery is made up of a number of burial areas, with the earliest graves dating back to the 1870s. The Odd Fellows started the cemetery with a bit of land purchased from Nils Peterson. Next, members of the Free Methodist Church and Cross & Company purchased the remaining land from Peterson to develop their personal burying spot. Ownership of the various portions of the cemetery has changed hands over the years. James W. Clise set up the Mount Pleasant Cemetery Company in 1895. Clise purchased the land from Cross & Company, but a number of churches and ethnic groups continued to maintain individual portions of the cemetery. The congregation Chaveth Sholem began the first Jewish cemetery in Seattle in Mount Pleasant Cemetery in 1890. In 1929 Temple de Hirsch obtained a portion of Mount Pleasant for the Hills of Eternity Jewish Cemetery. Today, Mount Pleasant is owned and operated by the Edwards family, who purchased it from Clise in 1957. Covering more than forty acres, Mount Pleasant holds thousands of graves, including those of a number of interesting persons. William and Sarah Bell (two of Seattle's pioneers), Rev. Daniel Bagley (advocate for Territorial University, later University of Washington), Opal Charmaine Mills (murder victim of the Green River Killer), some

MOUNT PLEASANT

of the unclaimed victims of the 1910 Wellington train disaster, and some of the ashes of songwriter Joe Hill are buried here. Late at night many passersby have heard what they describe as a baby crying. As they would look around to find where they crying was coming from, no source could be found. Or the crying would stop before they got closer.

See also: Methodist Church in Capitol Hill

CALVARY

5041 Thirty-fifth Avenue NE

Dedicated in 1889, Calvary was the city's first major Catholic cemetery, with over forty thousand buried here on this forty-acre plot on the southwest slope of a hill overlooking University Village. This location also includes Union and Confederate veterans of the Civil War and refugees from the war in Vietnam along with a strong Catholic community. The oldest burial space at Calvary belongs to William Boyd who died in 1859. Boyd was originally buried in the old Seattle Cemetery before it was converted into a park. His remains were moved to The Holy Cross Cemetery on Capitol Hill before it was sold and the bodies were removed. Hopefully, he has now found his final resting spot here—until they decide to sell this cemetery or move him once more.

CALVARY

Some folks say they've seen a woman in a blue dress wandering this location. She always appears around dusk, just before the cemetery closes. Security has seen her a few times, believing she is a guest visiting a grave, but when they go to inform her that the cemetery is closed, she disappears without a trace.

See also: Denny Park in Belltown; Seattle Preparatory School in Capitol Hill

FOREST LAWN
6701 Thirtieth Avenue SW

Here you will find the grave of Patricia Barczak, who was murdered by Gary Leon Ridgway, the Green River serial killer, in 1986. He raped, strangled, and dumped bodies near the Green River. He was finally caught in 2003 and confessed to approximately fifty murders. Barczak's remains were not found until 1993. Also, Denise Naslund is buried here. She was murdered by serial killer Ted Bundy in 1974. Naslund disappeared from Lake Sammamish State Park; her remains were found about two miles away. Bundy confessed to her murder shortly before his execution. Many believe that

FOREST LAWN

those who die violently at someone else's hands, tend to hang around this world until their killer has been brought to justice. Prior to Bundy being caught, many felt that the spirits of his victims walked these grounds in search of him.

CROWN HILL

8712 12th Avenue NW

This ten-acre cemetery was founded in 1903 by civic leaders in the town of Ballard. It is believed to be haunted by the sounds of old man Sharpnack's creaking wheelchair. The legend is that in 1916 he was buried upright, sitting in his wheelchair, in the mausoleum that was built for him according to directions left after he committed suicide. A man is also seen pacing back and forth, and he seems to be guarding certain areas of the cemetery. Walking through the cemetery, people often get the sense that they are being followed or even watched.

CROWN HILL

FORT LAWTON

3801 W Government Way

Founded in 1896 by the U.S. Army, the fort opened in 1900 on eleven hundred acres. Named after Maj. Gen. Henry Ware Lawton, the fort was redesigned in 1902 for infantry use. In 1938 the Army offered to sell the fort back to the city of Seattle for just one dollar, but the city declined because of maintenance concerns. At least twenty thousand troops were stationed at the fort during World War II. The base was also used as a prisoner-of-war camp, with over one thousand Germans imprisoned there.

On August 15, 1944, Guglielmo Olivotto, an Italian POW, was murdered at the fort after rioting between American soldiers and Italian POWs. Twenty-eight African-American soldiers were later court-martialed, convicted, and sent to prison. In 2007 the convictions were overturned. A ceremony offering a formal apology from the U.S. Army was held in 2008 during which relatives of former soldiers and the two remaining survivors were presented with years of back pay following the overturn of their dishonorable discharges.

The land was given back to the city in 1972 and dedicated as Discovery Park in 1973. The grounds contain numerous historic buildings, structures, and a four-section military cemetery. The first bodies were laid to rest here in 1902, and the cemetery is now home to 911 others that have made this their final resting place.

Many have seen apparitions of military men wandering the old fort. If you visit on a calm and quiet night, you might hear the voices of the past talking among themselves. It is clear that some of these men feel the need to still stand guard over their beloved country.

See also: Lake View Cemetery and G.A.R. Cemetery in Capitol Hill;
Denny Park and The Josephinum in Belltown
Comet Lodge Cemetery in Georgetown
Seattle Preparatory School in Capitol Hill
Me-Kwa-Mooks Park in Seattle Parks
Fairmount Hotel in Waterfront and Downtown

FORT LAWTON

SPOOKED IN SEATTLE TOURS

Join real ghost hunters from AGHOST for an evening of adventure, as they take you on a guided tour of some of Seattle's most haunted sites. Each tour explores the past of some of the oldest buildings in Seattle. These two-hour walking tours explore ghosts, murder, the strange, and some of the evidence collected during paranormal investigations. You may leave wondering, "Are ghosts for real, or are we haunted by the spooks in our minds?" Come join us and see why we are "Spooked In Seattle."

For times and booking information:

(425) 954-7701; **www.spookedinseattle.com**

AGHOST

Twas a dark and stormy Night . . . in the year 2000. Halloween night, to be exact. Ross Allison, paranormal enthusiast, had convinced a group of his friends to do some late-night ghost hunting in a local cemetery. A chill wind blew down the deserted street and dead leaves whirled and flew through the air. As at last the cemetery gates loomed in the near distance, thunder boomed, lightening crashed, and a dismal rain began to fall. "Wow! That was pretty cool, huh guys?" exclaimed Ross. "Guys?" Turning, he saw the distant silhouettes of his friends, running as fast as they could in the opposite direction. Frustrated, Ross sighed, "Where can I get some people to go ghost hunting with?!?" It was at that moment AGHOST was born.

Over the years, AGHOST has investigated close to five hundred sites including private residences, colleges, castles, ships—the list goes on. Each client and location is treated with respect and care, as are those spirits they have encountered. It is not our role to do "ghost busting" but rather to detect if spirits are present and, if they are, to attempt communication with them. AGHOST's approach to clients and the general public is to educate them with regards to the paranormal while attempting to bridge the gap between fear and understanding. Education is key to the success of AGHOST, preceded in importance only by our dedication to obtaining as much factual, verifiable data as possible from the locations we investigate. We provide training to all registered members, review our data and report our findings, and take our findings to the general public in the form of lectures, classes and tours. Meetings and investigative services have always been and will continue to be free to the public. That we be allowed to seek out the paranormal where it is detected is our wish because, as Ross always says,

"The Truth will be found."

Learn more about Advanced Ghost Hunters Of Seattle—Tacoma, AGHOST Line (253) 203-4383; **www.aghost.org; angryghosthunters/blogspot.com**

GLOSSARY

Anomaly: Something which cannot be explained by currently accepted scientific theories.

Apparition: An unexpected or preternatural appearance; a ghost; a specter; a phantom. A rare photographic anomaly normally captured on film. An apparition is a ghost that has taken human form.

Apport: French word meaning, "to bring." This is where objects will appear out of nowhere. Phenomena related to spirits interacting with the living.

Asport: French word meaning, "to send." Also known as Deporting, this is where objects will disappear or be moved from one location to another. Phenomena related to spirits interacting with the living.

Aura: A luminous radiation often reported around beings usually observed with special equipment or by a person with enhanced psychic ability.

Automatism: Automatic behavior or movement without consciousness or self-control

Automatic Writing: A form of spirit communication where the spirit takes control of the hosts hand to write messages while the host in in a trance like state.

Cleansing: A term used in spirit exorcism. The removing of the spirit from the property

Cold Spot: Where the temperature drops significantly in a certain place or location that it is noticed by human touch.

Collective Apparition: An apparition that is seen simultaneously by multiple witnesses.

Coupling: Using two different pieces of equipment or methods of research to verify paranormal phenomena.

Demonology: The practice that specializes in the removal of evil or demonic forces from a given environment. A belief that demonic forces are at fault or imitating the living.

Déjà vu: The experience that seems as if you are re-experiencing the event or situation that has appeared to have happened before.

Dream Communication: A method of communicating with the dead by interpreting dreams.

Ectoplasm: The substance supposed to emanate from the body of the medium during a trance. Usually resembles smoke or fog in photographs.

Electromagnetic Field: The field of force associated with electric charge in motion, having both electric and magnetic components and containing a definite amount of electromagnetic energy; believed to be generated when spirits manifest.

Electronic Voice Phenomenon (EVP): A phenomenon where voices or sounds are captured on a recording medium, usually a tape recorder. Often no sound is heard while the tape is recording but on playback distinct voices may be heard.

EMF Detector: An instrument for measuring the magnitude and direction of a magnetic field. Also known as a Gauss Meter or magnetometer.

Entity: A being or self contained bodiless form of existence, most commonly referred to as ghost or spirit.

Epicenter: The region that seems to be in the center of activity being investigated such as the focal area of ghostly activity.

ESP: Extra Sensory Perception The ability to perceive things outside the normal range of senses.

Extra Sensory: Residing beyond or outside the normal senses.

Ghost: A disembodied soul; especially, the soul of a dead person believed to be an inhabitant of the unseen world or to appear to the living in bodily likeness. The spirit of a dead person, especially one believed to appear in bodily likeness to living persons or to haunt former habitats. Soul, Spirit, Demon. The disembodied spirit of a dead person, conceived of an appearing to the living as a pale, shadowy apparition.

Ghost Light: An unexplainable light visible to the naked eye. It may be seen traveling in a conscious manner, giving the appearance of intelligence.

Ghost Hunt: Going to a place were there have been no sightings of ghosts and trying to catch some on film (video and photos), sounds, eyewitness, etc. (graveyards are the number one place to start, churches, schools and older buildings too).

Ghost Investigation: Going to a known haunted place and recording data (video, photos, audio, and temperatures), notes, interviews and other evidence to prove/disprove the haunting and to assist the owners and the spirits in moving on and leaving the place if they want that. The assistance can be either you directly assisting the owner with the situation or putting them in contact with experienced groups or individuals that will try to resolve the situation. Your assistance can be something as simple as educating them on what is going on and their options.

Haunt(ing/ed): A place, area, or building that exhibits ghostly apparitions or other signs of ghostly activity. Inhabited by, or subject to the visits of, apparitions; frequented by a ghost. Haunt: Visit often or continually. Frequented by ghosts.

Hoax: An act taken in an attempt to trick or dupe people or ghost hunters into believing that a place is haunted when there is no ghostly activity taking place.

Home Circle: A séance held in someone's home without the uses of a professional medium.

Intelligent Haunting: A spirit that interacts with its surroundings and with the living.

Manifestation: One of the forms in which someone or something, such as a divine being, is revealed; the materialized form of a spirit.

Medium: A person thought to have the power to communicate with the spirits of the dead or with agents of another world or dimension. Also called psychic.

Metaphysics: Derived from the Latin word Meta which means beyond. Literally means that which is beyond the laws of physics.

Mist: A photographed anomaly that appears as a wall of light that is not seen at the time of the photograph; believed to be the appearance of a ghost or spirit of the dead.

Orb: Glowing balls of light or energy that often accompany a haunting and show up on photographs. A photographed anomaly that appears as a ball of light and may occasionally seem to be moving that is not seen at the time of the photograph; believed to represents a ghost.

Ouija Board: A trademark used for a board with the alphabet and other symbols on it, and a planchette that is thought, when touched with the fingers, to move in such a way as to spell out spiritualistic and telepathic messages on the board.

Paranormal: Literally, beyond normal. An event or instance which cannot be explained using our natural or normal science or rationale.

Paranormal: Beyond the range of normal experience or scientific explanation.

Parapsychology: The study of the evidence for psychological phenomena, such as telepathy, clairvoyance, and psycho kinesis, that is inexplicable by science.

Percipient: Capable of perception; one who perceives

Phantom: Something apparently seen, heard, or sensed, but having no physical reality; a ghost or an apparition. Something that seems to appear to the sight but has no physical existence; Apparition, Vision, Specter. Something to be feared or dreaded.

Phenomena: A term used to describe anything that cannot be explained in scientific terms

Poltergeist: A ghost that manifests itself by noises, rappings, and the creation of disorder. Responsible for mysterious noisy disturbances or moving, misplacing of objects. Some poltergeists have been reported to cause physical harm to people.

Portal: A doorway to another dimension through which spirits, ghosts and other entities may be able to pass.

Possession: Spirit domination over the physical body

Provocation: This term is used to describe a method of provoking a response or action from the spirits.

PSI: A term used to describe any psychic ability

Psychic: A person apparently sensitive to non physical forces. Also referred to as a medium.

Psychic Chill: This is where a chill of cold ness will be felt, but there is no physical readings from tools to prove the phenomena.

Residual Haunting: A term used to describe energy that is trapped in a continuous loop.

Séance: A meeting normally conducted by a medium in an effort to receive spirit communications.

Shadow People: Unexplained shadows that appear in photographs and video, believed to be associated with evil or angry spirits or possessing negative energy. Some observers have reported seeing them with their naked eyes.

Sixth Sense: A term used to describe psychic ability. Sixth being outside the five common senses as in sight, touch, smell, taste and hear.

Skeptical: hesitating to admit the certainly of doctrines or principles; doubting of everything.

Spirit: An entity that has a consciousness and is able to interact with investigators that haunts an area

Spirit Photography: Photographs that contain images of the ghosts, writing, famous faces, or even strange light formations. Also known as extras.

Spiritualism: A religion that practices the beliefs that the soul survives bodily death and can communicate with the living through humans or mediums.

Supernatural: Not existing in nature or subject to explanation according to natural laws; not physical or material.

Vortex: A photographed anomaly that appears as a funnel or rope-like image that is not seen at the time of the photograph; believed to represents a 'ghost'

Wraith: Guardian; a ghost. Spectral figure of a person supposedly seen as a premonition just before that person dies.

OTHER RESOURCES
BOOKS:

Davis, Jefferson. *A Haunted Tour Guide to the Pacific Northwest*. Norsemen Ventures

Dwyer, Jeff. *Ghost Hunter's Guide to Seattle & Puget Sound*, Pelican Publishing

Ferguson, Robert L. *The Pioneers of Lake View*, Thistle Press

Hauck, Dennis William. *Haunted Places*, Penguin Books

Moffitt, Linda. *Washington's Haunted Hotspots*, Schiffer.

Rule, Leslie. *When the Ghosts Screams*. Andrews McMeel Publishing

Smith, Barbara. *Ghost Stories of Washington*, Lone Pine Publishing.

Speidel, Bill. *Sons of the Profits*, Nettle Creek.

ONLINE RESOURCES:

kingcounty.gov

georgetownhistory.com

seattle.gov

wikipedia.org

historylink.org

ACKNOWLEDGMENTS

Barbie Lumbert, Thanks for your years of support and assistances in research.

Jon Michael Allison-Murphy, For your, assistance, support, and checking over my writings.

Jody Cassady, Thanks for being the great woman behind the successful man.

Mercedes Yaeger at Market Ghost Tours, Thanks for the extra stories

Joe Teeples, for your assistance and co-authoring of *Ghostology 101*, you helped lead the way.

Jeff Davis, Your hard work and friendship is an inspiration to all ghost hunters.

TITLES IN THE AMERICA'S HAUNTED ROAD TRIP SERIES:

Ghosthunting Florida
Ghosthunting Kentucky
Ghosthunting Illinois
Ghosthunting Maryland
Ghosthunting New Jersey
Ghosthunting New York City
Ghosthunting North Carolina
Ghosthunting Ohio
Ghosthunting Ohio: On the Road Again
Ghosthunting Pennsylvania
Ghosthunting Southern New England
Ghosthunting Texas
Ghosthunting Virginia

Cincinnati Haunted Handbook
Haunted Hoosier Trails
More Haunted Hoosier Trails
Nashville Haunted Handbook

ABOUT THE AUTHOR

Ross Allison is the president and founder of AGHOST (Advanced Ghost Hunters of Seattle-Tacoma) with twenty years of experience investigating the paranormal and ten years of experience running a ghost hunting group. He travels internationally to investigate paranormal activity, collect ghost stories, and research cemeteries. He lectures to thousands of students at more than one hundred colleges and universities throughout the U.S. on ghost hunting adventures and teaches a class based on his book, *Ghostology 101: Becoming a Ghost Hunter,* at the University of Washington. He's appeared on a number of radio programs, in magazines, books, news coverage, and television shows, including The Learning Channel's America's *Ghost Hunters, The Tonight Show,* MTV, CMT, CNN, ABC's *Scariest Places on Earth,* SyFy's *Ghost Hunters, Nightline,* and two episodes of Travel Channel's *Most Terrifying Places in America.*

ROSS ALLISON

Ross also is the owner of Spooked in Seattle Tours, which last year drew more than 2,500 people and continues to grow every year. The tours are given by bus, by horse-drawn carriage, or on foot. Very popular with tourists, the tours also are attracting locals who want to find out more about the hauntings in the Emerald City. He lives in Tacoma, Washington.

Printed in the USA
CPSIA information can be obtained
at www.ICGtesting.com
JSHW012024140824
68134JS00033B/2861